"Thank you, Fynn, for creating such a special book on the importance of sibling relationships. Fynn's emphasis on play and multi-age learning as a driving force for curating a lifelong sibling bond is so valuable."

Susie Allison, author and creator of *Busy Toddler*

"This is a brilliant book. Fynn creates projects and activities that engage children's curious minds, build sibling relationships, foster creativity, and promote play. Fynn shows us how having fun and learning go hand in hand."

Autumn Vandiver, preschool teacher and parent coach
www.coachingwithautumn.com

"This book is an inspiring collection of practical and thoughtful activities for families to enjoy. I particularly love the quick and easy setups which help alleviate the pressures of coordinating activities for my children. This book has become a must-have in my family and I highly recommend it for yours."

Myriam Sandler, creator of *MOTHERCOULD*
www.mothercould.com

"An engaging book that helps children to learn important developmental and social skills while entertaining themselves. A must-have book to bring siblings together and reinforce their unbeatable bond (while giving busy parents a much needed break)."

Agnes Hsu, creator of kids craft site
www.hellowonderful.co

"Fynn is the best at creating simple, educational activities that siblings can do together at home. I love that this book allows all my kids to play and engage, while learning at their own pace."

Andrea Scalzo Yi, founder of RaisingDragons.com and author of *100 Easy STEAM Activities: Awesome Hands-On Projects for Aspiring Artists and Engineers*

"The ideas in this book are ingenious and you'll be left saying, 'Thanks, Fynn, for helping me create happy learners.'"

"Fynn's dedication to early childhood and sibling learning is breathtaking. Everything Fynn creates is thoughtfully designed to guide children through hands-on, inspiring play ideas."

"Fynn makes learning fun with 50 easy activities that use mostly common household items. I love that you can involve all of your kids to do them together."

"Fynn has written such a helpful resource for parents of toddlers through school-aged children. I would recommend this book to all moms like myself with multiple children at home."

"If you have multiple children, this is the book for you. Fynn does an amazing job of simplifying things for parents, in a smart and do-able way!"

The Happy Learning Book FOR SIBLINGS

50 Awesome Activities for Siblings to Learn and Play Together at Home

Fynn Sor

Creator of *Happy Tot Shelf*

WS Education

Published by

WS Education, an imprint of

World Scientific Publishing Co. Pte. Ltd.

5 Toh Tuck Link, Singapore 596224

USA office: 27 Warren Street, Suite 401-402, Hackensack, NJ 07601

UK office: 57 Shelton Street, Covent Garden, London WC2H 9HE

National Library Board, Singapore Cataloguing in Publication Data
Names: Sor, Fynn.
Title: The happy learning book for siblings : 50 awesome activities for siblings to learn and play together at home /
    Fynn Sor.
Description: Singapore : WS Education, [2020]
Identifiers: OCN 1157200354 | ISBN 978-981-122-434-8 (paperback) | 978-981-122-416-4 (hardcover)
Subjects: LCSH: Child rearing. | Brothers and sisters--Recreation. | Learning. | Play.
Classification: DDC 649.1--dc23

British Library Cataloguing-in-Publication Data
A catalogue record for this book is available from the British Library.

For any available supplementary material, please visit
https://www.worldscientific.com/worldscibooks/10.1142/11935#t=suppl

Printed in Singapore

To my hubby, Shuhong,
who is my biggest cheerleader,
and to my three children,
Zachary, Riley, and Abby,
whose playfulness and curiosity
inspire everything I do.

Contents

Chapter Six

Chapter Seven

Chapter Eight

Disclaimer: All the activities featured in this book require adult supervision. Adults should use their best judgement to minimise the risk of potential safety problems and to ensure appropriate use of all materials.

introduction

Sisters and brothers are the truest, purest forms of love, family and friendship, knowing when to hold you and when to challenge you, but always being a part of you.

Carol Ann Albright Eastman

Siblings are blessings. They are one of the best gifts we can give to our children.

I have three children and one of my biggest wishes, and probably yours too, is for our children to have many wonderful memories of growing up together.

In 2014, I started doing learning activities with my son Zachary, who is my eldest child, to nurture his love of learning and to spend quality time together. While these reasons still motivate me to organise activities for my children, our activity time took on a new focus when his little sisters, Riley and Abby, came along. Through learning and playing together, my children and I build strong connections with each other. And, they nurture healthy sibling relationships with each other.

With siblings in the picture, the way we did activities changed completely. Since they are of different ages, they have vastly different abilities and learning needs. As a mother of three young children, I am also more time-strapped than ever. These new challenges did not deter me from putting together activities for my children. On the contrary, I became motivated to create multi-age activities that engaged all my children and required as little preparation time as possible.

Through numerous conversations with other moms, I quickly realized that there are many like me out there who are looking for simple fun activities for siblings. I am passionate about helping fellow busy parents raise happy learning siblings, and that is how this book came to be.

How to Use this Book

In this book, you will find 50 tried and tested, easy and fun activities, all of which have been approved by my in-house activity testers. Every activity is designed for siblings to have fun at home and uses mostly common household items or craft materials. There are step-by-step instructions, vivid photographs, and ideas to adapt the activity for older or younger siblings.

The 50 activities are grouped under five main learning areas:

- Literacy
- Numeracy
- Discovery of the World
- Motor Skills
- Sensory Play, Arts and Crafts

Every activity comes with ideas on how to adapt the set-up or materials for three age groups:

- Toddlers (2 to 3 years old),
- Preschoolers (3 to 6 years old), and
- School-aged Kids (6 to 9 years old)

While I give recommended ages throughout the book, feel free to pick what's most suitable for your children's skill levels and interests. You know your children best.

This book is designed to get your children (and you!) started on learning and playing together. Flip through this book and choose your next family activity within these pages!

I hope these activities will give your children countless hours of engaging fun and beautiful childhood memories with their siblings.

Chapter 1

The Benefits of Positive Sibling Relationships

> Siblings are the people we practise on, the people who teach us about fairness and cooperation and kindness and caring — quite often the hard way.
>
> **Pamela Dugdale**

had my second child, Riley, when I was already knee-deep into caring for Zachary, my then super-clingy two-year-old son.

Four years later, Abby joined our chaotic family, and before you know it, skip to the present and it's dawned on me that I've pretty much been dealing with night feeds and diapers for the past half a decade or so! Nevertheless, looking back at those bleary-eyed years with young children, I don't regret the struggles because I now see the magic of having siblings and all the benefits that come with positive sibling relationships.

Benefits of Growing up with Siblings

When younger siblings interact with their older siblings, they may pick up more advanced language and this usually translates into better communication skills and play skills.

Younger siblings are also likely to be more adventurous and open to new experiences if they have an older sibling, whom they usually look up to as a role model. With an older sibling, our younger children learn more and engage in more advanced activities than they would be capable of doing on their own.

My second child, Riley, surprised me when she learned to ride a bicycle when she was three. I guess she wanted to catch up with her big brother! And, as for Abby, my third child, she started crawling at four months old, the earliest of my three children!

There are many benefits for older siblings as well. Through caring for their younger siblings, older children learn to nurture and lead. They also tend to be more patient and sensitive to others around them because of the caregiving role they take on with their younger siblings. Older siblings get to practise these skills, which are all essential life skills in order to be good parents and leaders once they're adults. It's no wonder that older siblings are more likely to grow up to be responsible and reliable.

As an added bonus to these essential caregiving skills, playing with younger siblings seems to bring out more creativity in older children. Once, I invited then three-year-old Riley and five-year-old Zachary to create a collage using cardboard cutouts. Zachary created a prim and proper flower while Riley created, in her words, a "powerful machine".

Zachary saw what his little sister had made and, inspired by her creativity, he went on to create his own "powerful machine" too.

Nurturing healthy connections among my children has become one of my top parenting goals because I am aware of the profound and enduring impact they can have on each other. Sibling relationships will probably be the longest lasting relationship my children have in their lives. Through their daily interactions, siblings are constantly shaping each other's identities and hopefully, making each other better persons.

While we know the benefits that come with positive sibling relationships, most parents wonder: *how do we create and nurture such relationships?*

One of the simplest ways to do that is to provide children with plenty of opportunities to learn and play *together*.

Chapter 2

The Basics of a Good Multi-age Learning Activity

Siblings who learn and play together, stay together. Activity time offers ideal opportunities for siblings to engage fully with one another.

Siblings are often a child's first playmate. All the time spent learning and playing together helps siblings to cultivate important social skills, such as cooperation, respecting and understanding each other's differences, sharing, and taking turns. Naturally, siblings will fight and bicker, but these moments give them opportunities to develop conflict resolution skills and empathy as they try to understand one another's point of view.

With their different ages, siblings have vastly diverse abilities and learning needs, which means what they are able to do and what they deem fun will vary.

No wonder I hear this question from parents all the time: "I don't know what activity to do for all my kids. What can they do together?"

To answer this question, we first need to understand what makes an activity engaging for children of different ages.

Open-ended vs Close-ended Activities

Broadly speaking, there are two types of structured activities adults can create for children: open-ended and close-ended activities.

A close-ended activity has exact steps to follow to achieve a fixed or predetermined outcome. Examples of close-ended activities would be playing a board game together or creating a craft where children have to follow the directions given. It is challenging to make close-ended activities work for siblings because it may be too difficult for younger siblings or too easy for older kids. Either way, one child will quickly lose interest.

On the flip side, open-ended activities have no fixed outcome. There are no right or wrong ways to complete the tasks. The process is child-led so children can freely direct the activity based on their creativity, imagination, and abilities. This freedom makes open-ended activities a great choice for children of different ages to do together.

For example, once, I invited my then three-year-old Riley and five-year-old Zachary to create and paint imaginary planets. Even with the same set up and

materials, the final products my children created were entirely different.

Here is a summary of the differences between open-ended and close-ended activities:

Open-ended activity	Close-ended activity
There is no fixed outcome	The outcome is predetermined
The process is child-led	The process follows exact steps
Encourages creativity and imagination	Develops mastery of certain skills
Ideal for children of diverse ages and abilities	Ideal for children of similar ages and abilities

Multiple Learning Levels

Activities involving multiple learning levels work great for siblings because they allow kids to contribute based on what they know and are good at. Older children can take on tasks that demand more advanced skills while younger children can work on simpler tasks that require basic skills.

For example, when making homemade play dough together, the smaller ones can help with mixing or pouring the ingredients while the bigger kids can measure and scoop out the precise amount of ingredients.

Everyone gets to participate and contribute.

Make it Fun

Kids (and adults) love having fun. So, incorporating fun into learning activities and playtime is one of the easiest ways to encourage siblings to play and learn together. When siblings share laughter and silliness, they build strong bonds that may last a lifetime as they create wonderful childhood memories.

Once, I set up the Alphabet Neighborhood (p. 20) activity for my then four-year-old daughter, Riley. As soon as I added a fun component where she had to hunt for the letters, my then six-year-old son Zachary wanted to join us. My children had so much fun, they played five rounds and asked for more. In fact, this activity undoubtedly deserves a top spot in our sibling activities list.

Adaptability to Other Skill Levels

There are some activities that are easily adaptable for different age groups. These are good options when you wish to teach children of different age groups different concepts using the same set up.

For example, in the Ultimate Shape Hunt (p. 54) game, younger kids look for different shapes and mark them by color while older siblings count the number of shapes and create a graph based on the data.

Since many younger siblings love to do what their big brother or sister is doing, you can easily adapt this activity to create an easier version for your younger child.

In the Alphabet Neighborhood (p. 20) activity, six-year-old Zachary matched uppercase letters to lowercase letters, e.g., 'A' to 'a'. For this activity to be appropriate for four-year-old Riley, I wrote another set of uppercase letters on sticky notes and invited her to match uppercase letters to each other, e.g., 'A' to 'A'. Same game, but adapted for each child's skill level and knowledge.

Conclusion

For an activity to pass the Perfect-For-Siblings test, you need at least one or more of the elements listed above present. Of course, the more elements you can incorporate into an activity, the higher the success rate of engaging all your children.

You'll know if you've succeeded if they ask to do the activity again. In fact, we have repeated the activities in this book several times and that's how they have made it to our top 50 list!

Chapter 3

More Tips for Learning and Playing with Siblings

Before diving into the list of 50 awesome activities, here are more tips for navigating activity time with siblings.

Respecting Differences and Personal Space

Sibling closeness is great, but we must remember our children are individual beings who have unique preferences, interests, and strengths.

To support these differences, rotate the activities based on your children's preferences. Encourage your children to take turns to decide which sibling learning activity to do. The child making the choice will feel proud his opinion is being valued. For the children who have to wait for their turn, they will learn to respect the fact that others have opinions that may be different from their own.

In addition, recognise that children may sometimes prefer to be alone and have their own personal time and space. In our home, my children's beds are their special space where they can have some alone time.

Scheduling Family Time

Often, our children's calendars are stuffed with school, enrichment programs and extra lessons. Siblings may hardly have time to see each other, let alone play together. I encourage parents to create a common time for their children to hang

out, play, or simply relax together. This time is important for our children to be children, and to create childhood memories with their siblings.

Here's how you can do this: Find a time where all your children are available and declare it Family Fun Time. Protect this special block of time as much as possible. If you can, put down your handphone, stop doing the housework, and join your children. Then, find an activity from this book and have fun together! Whether it's 15 minutes or one hour, spending time together on a regular basis goes a long way toward building stronger family and sibling bonds.

Activity Time with a Baby

This activity guide was written for siblings with ages ranging from two years old to nine years old. Activities for babies and young toddlers under two years old were not included for developmental and safety reasons.

However, with parental guidance, some of these activities can be simplified using baby-safe materials whenever possible.

For example, when six-year-old Zachary and four-year-old Riley were painting in our bathroom shower stall with tempera paint (which is not safe for a baby), I gave Abby, who was then just a baby, a clean brush and some water in a paint cup outside the shower area. This allowed my littlest one to engage in a similar but age-appropriate activity, while observing and enjoying the colors her older siblings used in their painting.

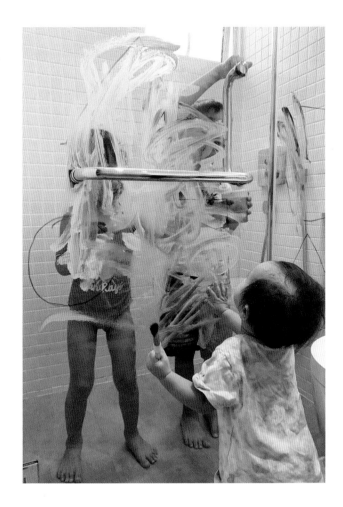

Activity Time with Big Kids

Children of all ages need a good amount of autonomy and as they grow older, this desire for autonomy becomes stronger. Big kids will start to express strong preferences in the food they eat, outfits they wear, videos they watch, and even activities they participate in. As parents, we want to nurture their confidence as they practise being autonomous and making decisions independently in their daily life.

During an activity, let your big kid direct the process as much as possible. Open-ended activities offer endless possibilities, so give your big kid the room they need for experimenting and exploring. When my seven-year-old joined in our Aluminum Alphabet

(p. 30) activity, he clearly had a mind of his own. He wrote the word 'zombie' and to be honest, I wasn't fond of his choice of word. But I chose to be open to his playful idea and not let my preference dictate the activity. The result? My son enjoyed the activity thoroughly because he had absolute ownership of the process and his creation. The sign now sits proudly on his bedroom door.

Chapter 4

Literacy

L iteracy is the ability to read with understanding and to write effectively to convey ideas and thoughts. Literacy development begins way before children enter school. At home, one of the easiest ways to enrich your children's literacy experience is to read to them daily. All children love a good story, and books are wonderful ways to bring families together. You can further nurture your children's early literacy skills through playful activities that lay the groundwork for writing and reading. The ten activities in this chapter offer creative ideas to encourage alphabet knowledge, phonological awareness, and writing.

The Alphabet Mystery Box (p. 26) is a simple crowd pleaser. Children get to use their sense of touch as they search for letters in the box. The Magic Letter Search (p. 36) is another delightful one to help children learn letters and sight words, and it uses a regular household item — paper towels! Or, make some Aluminum Alphabet (p. 30) together. Children can hone their fine motor skills as they roll and twist aluminum foil to make the letters of the alphabet.

Which activity will you and your children try today?

Alphabet Neighborhood

Using sticky notes, this activity is an easy way to encourage letter recognition.

How to set up this activity for preschoolers

- Draw 26 houses and write uppercase letters A to Z on the roofs.

- Write uppercase letters A to Z on the sticky notes.

- Invite your preschooler to match the letters on the sticky notes with those on the houses.

- This can be easily changed to an uppercase-to-lowercase-letters matching activity by simply writing lowercase letters a to z on the sticky notes.

Prep time

10 mins

Clean-up time

5 mins

Materials

· Sticky notes · Big pieces of paper · Markers

How to simplify this activity for toddlers

- Draw the number of houses that corresponds to the number of letters in your child's name. Write the letters of your child's name on the houses and sticky notes. Invite your toddler to match the letters to form his name.

- For young toddlers who are not interested in letters yet, change this into a color-matching activity. Color the roofs and the sticky notes with the following colors: red, orange, yellow, green, blue, and purple.

- Invite your toddler to match the colors on the sticky notes with those on the roofs.

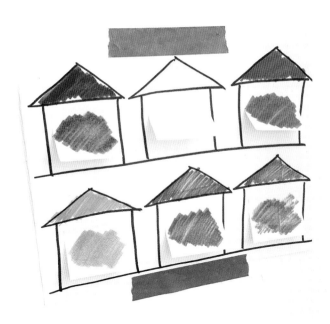

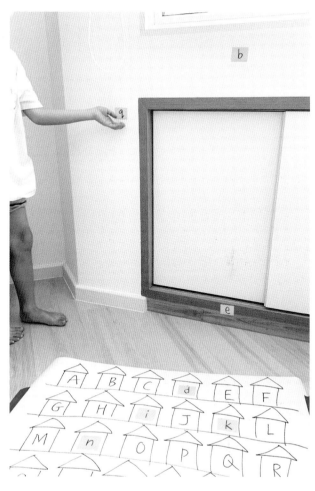

How to extend this activity for school-aged kids

- Invite your big kid to find toys and items around the house with the same beginning sounds as the letters on the houses. Work with her to spell out the names of the toys and items and write them down.

Tape Your Name

Children will absolutely love this hands-on and creative way to learn their names.

How to set up this activity for preschoolers

- Invite your child to write his name on the paper.

- If your preschooler is not writing yet, write his name in pencil and invite him to trace over it with a marker.

- Ask your child to cut small pieces of washi tape and paste them along the lines of the letters.

- Lastly, paint over the name and the entire piece of paper. When the paint dries, carefully peel off the tape to reveal his name.

Prep time
10 mins

Clean-up time
10 mins

Materials
· Paper · Washi tape · Paint
· Scissors · Brushes · Marker

How to simplify this activity for toddlers

- Write your toddler's name on the paper.

- Toddlers may not be skilled in cutting tape yet. You can help your toddler by pre-cutting small pieces of tape and sticking them on the edge of the table. Your toddler can help himself to these pre-cut tapes for the activity.

- Tip: Dot paint markers or paint sticks are toddler-friendly paint options.

How to extend this activity for school-aged kids

- Invite your big kid to get creative with the font or the letters.

- She may write her name in other interesting fonts, like cursive or bubble, or choose to use a different word.

Invisible Letters

This invitation to learn combines a classic watercolor and crayon-resist activity with letters or sight words recognition.

Tip

No liquid watercolor? You can make some with food coloring and water.

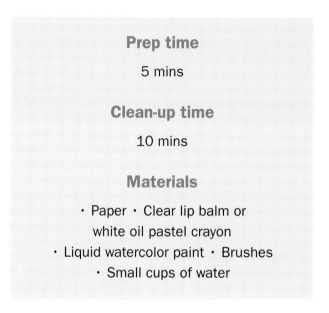

Prep time

5 mins

Clean-up time

10 mins

Materials

· Paper · Clear lip balm or white oil pastel crayon
· Liquid watercolor paint · Brushes
· Small cups of water

How to set up this activity for preschoolers

• Write the letters A to Z on paper with the clear lip balm. Invite your child to paint over the paper with watercolor to reveal the letters. As each letter is revealed, encourage your children to call out the letter names or sounds.

Using the clear lip balm, write uppercase letters and lowercase letters on two separate pieces of paper. Invite your preschooler to reveal the uppercase and lowercase letters, and match them together.

How to simplify this activity for toddlers

- Write several of the same letter on the paper with the lip balm.

- Tell your toddler that he's going to make a letter appear all over the paper.

- Invite him to find the letters by painting over the paper with watercolor.

How to extend this activity for school-aged kids

- Write a secret message for your big kid. Invite her to paint over the paper with watercolor. Read the secret message aloud.

- Invite your big kid to write a secret message for you or her younger siblings.

Variation for school-aged kids

Using the clear lip balm, write sight words on the paper.

Invite your big kid to paint over and reveal each sight word, then read it out for you and make a fun sentence with the word.

Alphabet Mystery Box

This is one activity that my children couldn't get enough of because it taps into their sense of curiosity as well as stimulates their sense of touch.

How to set up this activity for preschoolers

- Using the penknife, cut a hole in the box big enough for your child's hand to fit in.

- (optional) Create a flap over the hole so that your children are not able to peek into the box. This increases the fun mystery element of this game. Put the letter pieces into the box, along with other random small items.

Prep time

10 mins

Clean-up time

5 mins

Materials

- A big box · Letter puzzle pieces
· Random small items, e.g., socks, clothes, little toys, spoons, forks, and small balls
· Penknife (for adult use only)
· Small piece of paper (optional)
· Scissors (optional) · Tape (optional)

- Invite your child to put his hand into the mystery box and find a letter puzzle piece. When he finds a letter, encourage him to name the letter and the corresponding letter sound.

How to simplify this activity for toddlers

- Whenever your toddler picks out a letter, ask him to name the letter. If he does not know letter names or sounds yet, you can say the letter names or sounds, and ask your toddler to repeat after you.

How to extend this activity for school-aged kids

- Challenge your big kid by asking him to guess the letter before pulling it out of the box and list three words beginning with that letter.

Variations for everyone

Keep this mystery box and repeat the game on another day with these variations:

- Siblings take turns to create a mystery box for each other. Ask one child to put five toys and other random items in the box. He calls out one toy and his sibling finds it.

- Use number puzzle pieces, or items of one particular shape (e.g., circle). Siblings take turns to find all the circular items in the mystery box.

Collage Letter Art

In this Art meets Literacy project, let your children's creativity take over and be amazed with what they can come up with!

How to set up this activity for preschoolers

- Ask your child to choose a few letters, e.g., the first letter or all the letters in his name. Draw the chosen letters in huge block or bubble letter font on the paper.

- Invite your child to decorate his block letters with the available art supplies.

Prep time
10 mins

Clean-up time
10 mins

Materials
· Paper · Any of the following art materials: washable markers, crayons, paint, dot paint markers, stickers, old magazines, etc.
· Glue · Scissors

How to simplify this activity for toddlers

- Provide toddler-friendly art supplies, like stickers, dot paint markers, and washable markers, for your toddler to decorate her block letters.

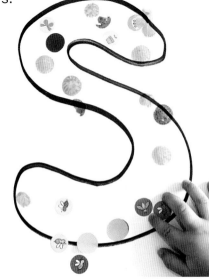

How to extend this activity for school-aged kids

- Ask your school-aged kid to find and cut pictures from old magazines that have the same beginning sound as her chosen letters.

- Invite her to use these to make collages within her letters.

Variation for everyone

Turn the letters into interesting three-dimensional assemblages with items found around the house. Siblings can collaborate and look for materials together. Some ideas include: bottle caps, pouch caps, buttons, straws, yarn, aluminum foil, etc.

Aluminum Alphabet

As children bend aluminum foil sticks to construct letters, the hands-on experience will reinforce their motor skills and help them learn letter formation.

Tip

No aluminum foil at home? Rolled-up magazine paper works well too.

How to set up this activity for preschoolers

- Demonstrate how to roll and twist aluminum foil into sticks. Invite your preschooler to make some sticks with aluminum foil.

Prep time

5 mins

Clean-up time

5 mins

Materials

- Sheets of aluminum foil
- Double-sided tape · Marker
- Rectangular pieces of cardboard

- Write the letters in her name on the piece of cardboard. Invite your child to use these aluminum foil sticks to form the letters. Use double-sided tape to stick the letters onto the cardboard.

How to simplify this activity for toddlers

- Write one letter on the cardboard. Make the letter as big as possible. Put double-sided tape on the letter and peel off the white backing.

- Roll some short aluminum foil sticks with your toddler. Shorter sticks are easier for your toddler to handle with her little hands.

- Invite your toddler to put the aluminum foil sticks on the lines to form the letter. Since there's double-sided tape on the letter, the toddler can focus on the letter formation.

How to extend this activity for school-aged kids

- Invite your big kid to get creative with the font or the word. He may write his name in other interesting fonts or choose to write a different word.

Variation for everyone

Make this a family project and create all the letters in the alphabet with aluminum foil sticks. These aluminum letters will make wonderful displays on the wall.

Fruity Names

Help your children learn how words are written while eating yummy fruits at the same time!

Tip

Do this activity during snack time. After the activity, your children can eat these healthy fruits.

Prep time

15 mins

Clean-up time

10 mins

Materials

- Various fruits cut into small pieces
- Clear glass baking dish or clear food container • Paper • Marker

How to set up this activity for preschoolers

- Write your child's name on a piece of paper. Write the name as big as possible.

- Place this paper under the clear baking dish.

- Invite your preschooler to trace his name with fruits.

How to simplify this activity for toddlers

- Draw some lines (straight, zigzag, wavy, etc) on a piece of paper and place it under the clear baking dish.

- Invite your toddler to trace these lines with fruits from left to right.

How to extend this activity for school-aged kids

- Ask your big kid to write his name as big as possible on a piece of paper.

- Invite him to trace his name with fruits.

- Challenge him to create some beautiful patterns while creating his name with fruits.

Book Makers

Blank books are one of the best ways to bring to life the thoughts and imagination of children.

Prep time

10 mins

Clean-up time

5 mins

Materials

· White paper · Colored paper
· Writing and drawing tools, like pencils, pens, markers, crayons, etc. · Stapler

How to set up this activity for preschoolers

- Invite your preschooler to stack three to five pieces of paper together and a piece of colored paper at the back.

- Fold the stack of paper into half such that the colored paper forms the book cover.

- Staple along the centerline to make a book.

- Encourage your preschooler to write or draw a story every day.

How to simplify this activity for toddlers

- Help your toddler make the book.

- Invite him to make marks and scribbles in his book every day.

How to extend this activity for school-aged kids

- Invite your school-aged kid to make a book on his own.

- Here are some ideas to use the book for your school-aged kid:

    1. Draw and write a comic
    2. Write a poem daily
    3. Write a journal to record his life for a week
    4. Draw and write about imaginary creatures
    5. Look out the window and draw and write what he observes

Variation for everyone

Make a yearly family journal book. Every family member gets to write or draw in this book. Here's how young toddlers can join in: encourage them to dictate their stories while you or an older sibling help pen down their exact words.

Magic Letter Search

Children will be fascinated to see letters appearing on a paper towel with their 'magic' touch!

Tip

Air-dry the paper towels and they can be reused several more times.

How to set up this activity for preschoolers

- Write the letters A to Z on a piece of paper.
- Write the letters A to Z with the permanent marker on a paper towel.
- Put another paper towel on top to cover the letters.

Prep time

10 mins

Clean-up time

5 mins

Materials

· Paper towels · Permanent marker
· Paper · Small cup of water

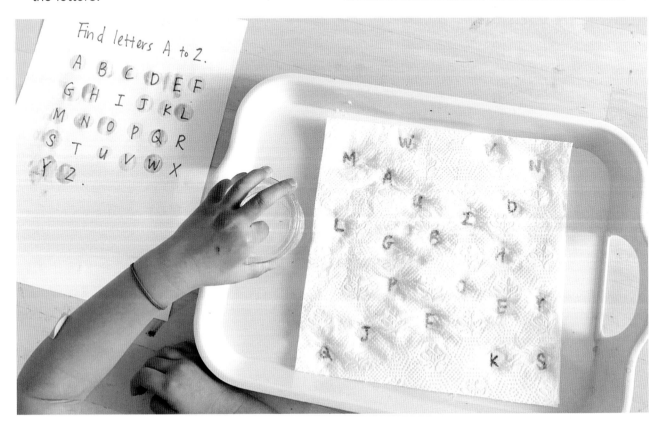

- Invite your preschooler to dap one finger into the water and dap the wet finger on the paper towel. The part of the paper towel that is wet will become see-through to reveal the letters behind. Ask your child to identify the letters that appear and cross them out on the paper.

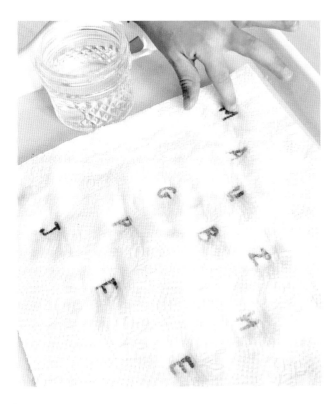

Variation for preschoolers

Try doing uppercase and lowercase letter-matching. Write the lowercase letters on the paper towel and the uppercase letters on the piece of paper.

How to simplify this activity for toddlers

- For toddlers, instead of writing A to Z, choose just one letter, e.g., B. Write many 'B's all over the paper towel.

- Let your child know that she is looking for letter B.

- Invite your toddler to find the letters by dabbing the paper towel with her wet finger.

How to extend this activity for school-aged kids

- Instead of letters, write sight words on the paper towel.

- Invite your school-aged kids to reveal and read out all the sight words on the paper towel. You can search the Internet for lists of sight words based on your child's academic level.

Family Post Box

By writing letters to family members and friends, children will see how their words and drawings convey their ideas to other people.

Prep time

10 mins

Clean-up time

10 mins

Materials

· An empty cereal box · Small pieces of paper or cards · Envelopes (optional) · Writing and drawing tools, like pencils, pens, markers, crayons, etc. · Stickers · Painter's tape

- Invite your children to write simple letters or draw pictures to everyone in the family. Provide envelopes for their letters. Encourage your preschooler to sign off the letter with her name and write the name of the recipient on the envelope.

- When they are done, drop the letters into the post box. Your children can take turns daily to be the postman and send out the letters.

How to set up this activity for preschoolers

- Make a flap at the top of the box by cutting across one long side and two short sides of the box (see photo). Cut a hole in the middle of the box. This is where the letters go in.

- Secure the post box on the wall with painter's tape.

How to simplify this activity for toddlers

- Provide toddler-friendly supplies and invite your toddler to decorate her cards with scribbles and stickers. Toddlers will love posting their cards into the post box again and again.

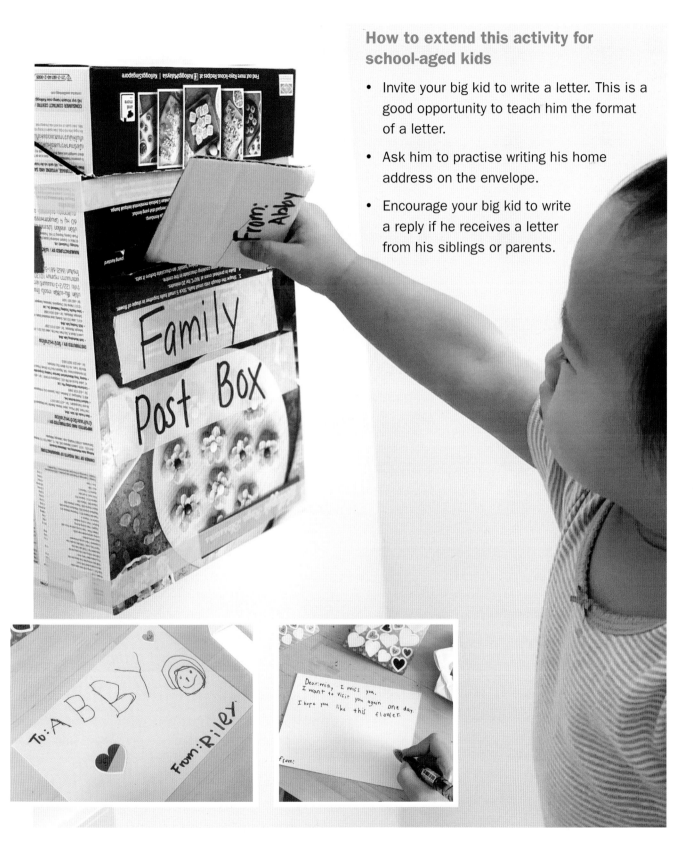

How to extend this activity for school-aged kids

- Invite your big kid to write a letter. This is a good opportunity to teach him the format of a letter.

- Ask him to practise writing his home address on the envelope.

- Encourage your big kid to write a reply if he receives a letter from his siblings or parents.

Chapter 5

Numeracy

Early positive experiences in mathematics set the stage for your children to develop confidence in mathematics and hopefully, love for this subject. To help our children make the connection between numeracy and the real world, weave math into their daily life and play so that they can see math being used in real life contexts. The ten hands-on activities in this section are great for children to explore numeracy concepts and skills through fun games and meaningful applications.

In Missing Number Hunt (p. 44), siblings play a fun game to find the missing numbers and complete their number sequences. Toys in a Pillowcase (p. 46) is another amazing activity for children to practise estimation and counting. The best part of this activity? Almost no preparation is needed. The Numbered Grid (p. 56) activity combines gross motor skills and numeracy and is our absolute favorite family activity.

Are you ready for some number fun? One, two, three. Let's go!

How Tall are You?

This easy activity introduces children to the concept of standard and non-standard units of measurement.

Prep time

1 min

Clean-up time

1 min

Materials

- As many pieces as possible of the same item, e.g., building blocks, magnetic tiles, spoons, coffee sachets, markers, and popsicle sticks
- Paper • Marker
- Ruler or measuring tape

How to set up this activity for preschoolers

- Let your children know that they are measuring each other's heights with magnetic tiles as shown in the photos. Ask them to guess the height of each family member based on the number of tiles used.

- Ask one child to lie down on the floor and a sibling to line up the magnetic tiles beside her, from head to toe.

- Count the number of tiles used together. Encourage everyone to point at each tile as they count and practise one-to-one correspondence counting.

Tip

Repeat this activity every few months and see how much your children have grown!

- Model the way to express the heights with non-standard units of measurement, e.g., say: "Riley is 15 tiles long."

- Every child takes turns to have their height measured with the tiles.

How to simplify this activity for toddlers

- Count the tiles together with your toddler. Point at each tile as she counts along with you.

- Ask these questions to explore comparative vocabulary and simple relationships between things: Who is the tallest? Who is the shortest? Who is taller or shorter than your brother/sister?

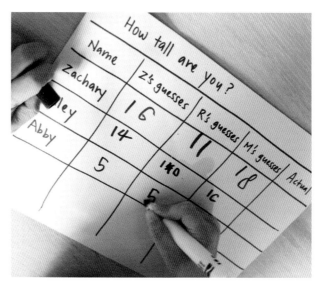

How to extend this activity for school-aged kids

- Encourage your big kid to record the number of tiles used for each family member in a table.

- Use a ruler or measuring tape to measure the height of each family member in standard unit of measurements like centimeters or inches.

- Contrast the heights measured with the ruler or measuring tape to that measured with the magnetic tiles.

Variation for school-aged kids

Invite your big kid to make his own ruler. Prepare a long strip of paper. Ask him to choose an item, like a spoon, as his unit of measurement.

Using the spoon, make regular marks and write numbers along the strip of paper, then invite your big kid to use his new ruler and measure the lengths of things he can find at home.

Variations for everyone

Invite your children to bring out their toys and measure their lengths with the tiles.

Or, get everyone to work together to measure the dimensions of a room with tiles.

Missing Number Hunt

This game is wonderful for practising counting, developing number recognition, and learning number sequences.

Prep time

5 mins

Clean-up time

1 min

Materials

· Sticky notes · A long piece of paper or several pieces attached together to form one long piece
· Marker

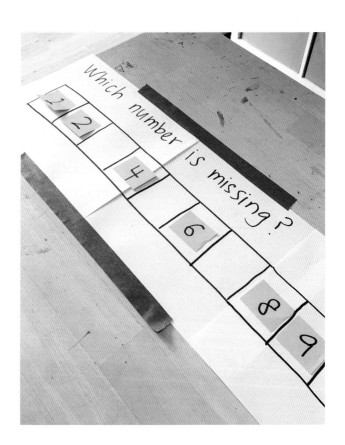

How to set up this activity for preschoolers

- Write numbers '1' to '10' on sticky notes

- Draw 10 boxes in a straight line. Each box must be big enough to fit a sticky note.

- Place the 10 sticky notes into the 10 boxes in sequence.

- Ask your preschooler to close her eyes. Remove a few sticky notes and get a sibling to hide them around the room.

- Ask your preschooler to figure out which numbers are missing and find the sticky notes. When she finds a sticky note, place it in the correct box.

Variation for preschoolers

Repeat this as many times as she wishes with these more challenging variations:

1. Remove more numbers

2. Rearrange the numbers in the boxes so that they are not arranged in sequence

3. Add numbers '11' to '20'.

How to simplify this activity for toddlers

- Write numbers '1' to '10' in the boxes. Invite your toddler to do number matching with the sticky notes.

How to extend this activity for school-aged kids

- Use multiples of a number to help your child learn skip counting and the times tables.

Variation for school-aged kids

Here are two more challenging variations to try:

1. Use your mobile phone number.

2. Draw a 5 by 6 grid with 30 boxes for 30 numbers.

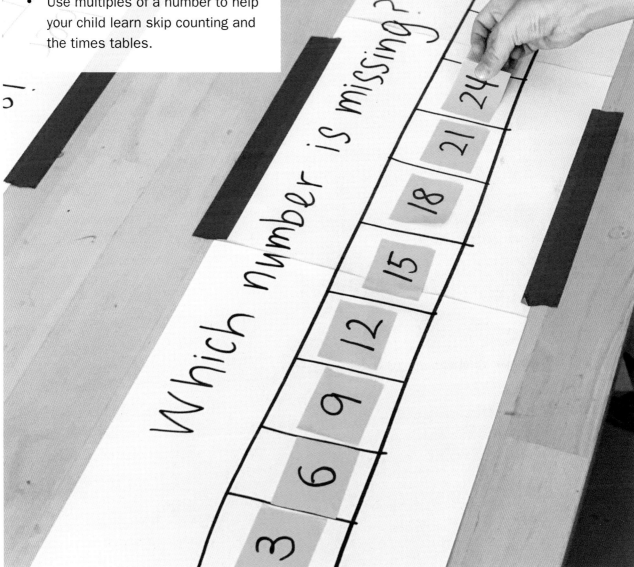

Toys in a Pillowcase

Through this easy game, children develop important skills of estimation and one-to-one correspondence counting!

Prep time

1 min

Clean-up time

1 min

Materials

· A pillowcase · Stuffed toys

How to set up this activity for preschoolers

- Task your child to put some stuffed toys into a pillowcase. The rest of the family should be outside the room.

- Everyone enters the room and takes turns to hold the pillowcase and guesses how many soft toys there are inside.

- Ask your child to empty the contents of the pillowcase and count the number of soft toys together.

How to simplify this activity for toddlers

- Hold the pillowcase open for your toddler as he puts stuffed toys into the pillowcase.

- During the reveal, task your toddler to take the stuffed toys out one at a time, while counting along with you.

How to extend this activity for school-aged kids

- Task your big kid to record everyone's guesses and the actual number.

- Challenge your big kid to practise subtraction to find out which siblings' guess was closest to the actual number.

Variation for school-aged kids

When taking out the toys to count, invite your big kid to count in multiples of 2, 5 or 10, to help him practise his times tables.

Number Houses

Another easy counting activity with sticky notes, because there's just something so entertaining about these small pieces of sticky paper.

Prep time

10 mins

Clean-up time

1 min

Materials

· Sticky notes · Huge pieces of paper
· Marker · Stickers

How to set up this activity for preschoolers

- Draw six big houses as shown in the picture. Divide each house into four equal parts. Each part needs to be big enough to fit a sticky note.

- Write numbers '1' to '6' on the six roofs.

- Write numbers '1' to '6' on six sticky notes.

- Draw one to six dots, lines, and triangles on eighteen sticky notes.

- Place these 24 sticky notes around the table or the room. Invite your preschooler to count and match the number of symbols and the numbers on the sticky notes to that on the roof.

How to simplify this activity for toddlers

- Draw five to ten houses, each with a different number of 'rooms'. See pages 40 and 49 for examples of the houses. Invite your toddler to paste a sticker in each 'room'.

- As your toddler is pasting the stickers, highlight the numbers on the roofs, e.g., by saying: "There are three rooms in this house for three stickers."

How to extend this activity for school-aged kids

- Draw six big houses and write six different numbers on the roof. On the sticky notes, write simple math problems. Invite your big kid to solve these problems and paste the sticky notes on the houses where the correct answers are written.

Variation for everyone

Attach the activity paper on the wall. This gives children the chance to work on a vertical surface and strengthen their core muscles, develop spatial awareness, and improve their hand-eye coordination.

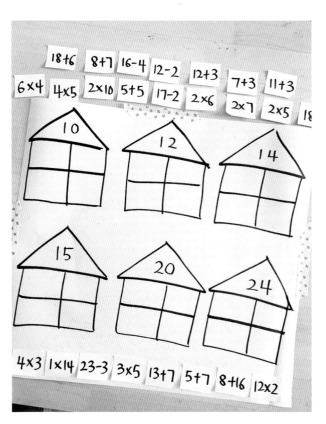

Measure the Lines

In this brilliant hands-on measuring activity, children get to engage their big muscles as they crawl on the floor and also work their small muscle groups as they lay the popsicle sticks along the lines. Double win!

Prep time

5 mins

Clean-up time

5 mins

Materials

· Painter's tape · As many pieces as possible of the same item, e.g., building blocks, magnetic tiles, spoons, coffee sachets, markers, and popsicle sticks · Ruler · Marker · Paper · Small toys or figurines

Tip

Keep these lines for Follow the Lines (p. 88).

How to set up this activity for preschoolers

- Using painter's tape, form three long lines on the floor. I made a straight line, a zigzag line, and a castle line (as shown in pictures).

- Ask your children to guess which line is the longest and which line is the shortest. Record their guesses.

- Task your children to measure these lines. Assign one line to each child, the straight line for the youngest and the castle line for the oldest.

- Invite your preschooler to line up the popsicle sticks along the line without leaving any gaps.

- Count how many popsicle sticks are used and record the number.

How to simplify this activity for toddlers

- Invite your toddler to use her favorite small toys or figurines and line them up on the lines. Tell her that the lines are bridges and her task is to help her toys cross the bridges safely.

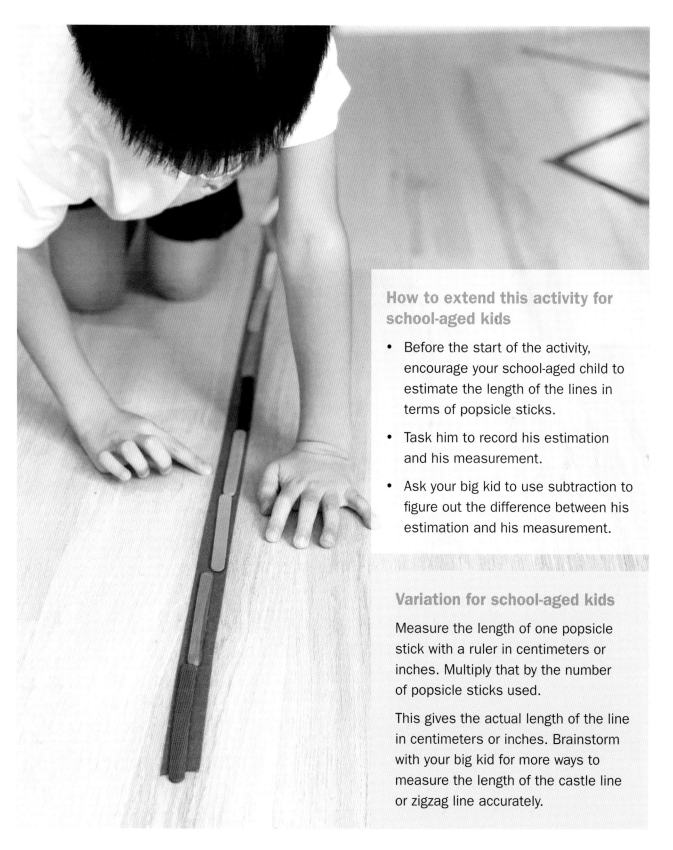

How to extend this activity for school-aged kids

- Before the start of the activity, encourage your school-aged child to estimate the length of the lines in terms of popsicle sticks.

- Task him to record his estimation and his measurement.

- Ask your big kid to use subtraction to figure out the difference between his estimation and his measurement.

Variation for school-aged kids

Measure the length of one popsicle stick with a ruler in centimeters or inches. Multiply that by the number of popsicle sticks used.

This gives the actual length of the line in centimeters or inches. Brainstorm with your big kid for more ways to measure the length of the castle line or zigzag line accurately.

Paper Cups Memory Game

This simple memory activity can hold your children's visual attention and help them learn a fundamental math concept, subitizing (the ability to instantly recognize a group of items without counting).

Prep time

5 mins

Clean-up time

5 mins

Materials

· 5 paper cups · Sticky notes
· Marker · 15 pom poms

How to set up this activity for preschoolers

- Put one, two, and three pom poms respectively under three overturned cups.

- Write numbers '1' to '3' on the sticky notes.

- Ask a sibling to move the overturned cups around one or two times to change their positions.

- Ask your preschooler to guess the number of pom poms in each cup by pasting the sticky notes on each cup.

- Reveal the answers by overturning the cups.

How to simplify this activity for toddlers

- Use two or three cups for your toddler. Place one pom pom under one cup.

- Move the overturned cups around once or twice and ask your toddler to guess which is the cup with the pom pom.

How to extend this activity for school-aged kids

- Use five cups and all 15 pom poms. Put one, two, three, four, and five pom poms respectively under each overturned cup.

- Ask a sibling to move the cups around three to five times. Then, conduct the rest of the game in the same way.

- An additional challenge for your big kid: You can give a mathematical problem with an answer between '1' to '5'. Ask your big kid to overturn the cup with the number of pom poms that matches the answer.

Ultimate Shape Hunt

In this collaborative shape hunt activity, siblings work together to search for and color code different basic shapes.

Prep time

10 mins

Clean-up time

1 min

Materials

· A huge piece of paper · Markers in five different colors · A black marker
· Shape Hunt Table printable on page 131
· Shape Hunt Graph printable on page 132
· Sticky notes or bottle caps

How to set up this activity for preschoolers

• Using the black marker, draw small circles, hearts, squares, rectangles, and triangles all over the paper.

• Task every child to find a shape and color the same shape in one color.

• After all the shapes are color coded, invite your preschooler to count the shapes and record the numbers in the Shape Hunt Table printable. For younger preschoolers, count along with them and provide help as they write the numbers.

• Extend the activity by inviting your preschooler to draw lines to connect the same shapes.

How to simplify this activity for toddlers

- Toddlers can join their older siblings to find and color/circle/point out a shape.

- After all the shapes are color coded, extend the activity by inviting your toddler to find and cover all of the shapes that you call out with bottle caps.

How to extend this activity for school-aged kids

- After all the shapes are color coded, invite your big kid to count the shapes and record the data in the Shape Hunt Graph printable.

- Invite your big kid to practise his addition and subtraction by giving him challenges like, "Add the number of circles and squares" or "Subtract the number of triangles from the number of hearts."

- Or, add more complicated shapes, e.g., pentagons, hexagons, semi-circles, and quarter-circles for your big kid to find and color.

Variation for everyone

Draw the shapes on sticky notes and stick them all over the house.

Assign each child to find all the sticky notes with a particular shape.

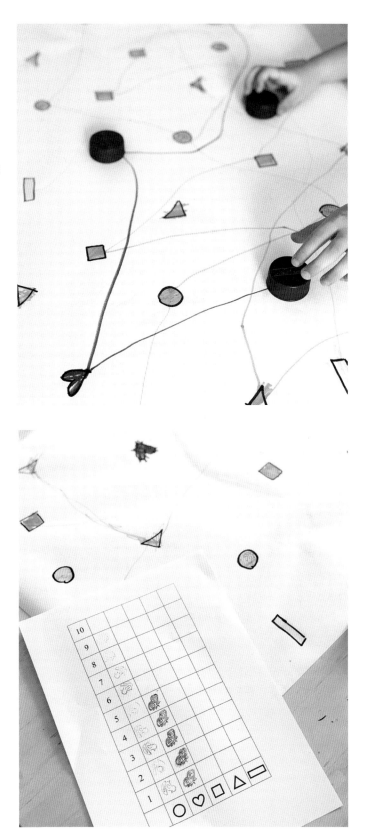

Numbered Grid

In our home, our numbered grid stayed on our floor for weeks and my children could not get enough of all the fun ways to play with it.

Prep time

15 mins

Clean-up time

10 mins

Materials

· Painter's tape
· 9 pieces of A6 paper
(A4 paper cut into four equal parts)
· Marker · 9 soft toys

How to set up this activity for preschoolers

- Make a huge 3 by 3 square grid on the floor with painter's tape.

- Write numbers '1' to '9' on the pieces of paper. Stick the numbers in each space using painter's tape.

- Make a start line with the painter's tape. Ask your children to stand or sit behind the start line.

- Call out a number and invite your preschooler to toss her soft toy into the box with that number. Return the soft toy to your child if it falls outside the box.

How to simplify this activity for toddlers

- Ask your toddler to stand just outside the grid.

- Call out and point at a number. Invite your toddler to toss a soft toy into the box with that number.

How to extend this activity for school-aged kids

- Instead of calling out numbers, give your big kid simple mathematical problems like 9 − 4, 2 + 4, 17 − 11 or 25 ÷ 5, etc. She will solve the problem and toss the toy to the box with the answer to the problem.

Variations for everyone

Here are three more fun ways to use this number grid:

1. Challenge everyone to find similar items that correspond to the numbers in the boxes.

2. Children take turns to call out the numbers or play in the grid. One child calls out a number and the other child jumps to it immediately. Or, get one of your children to call out two to three numbers at the same time. The other child touches all the numbers with her feet and hands as quickly as possible.

3. Play a giant tic tac toe game with the grid. Children take turns tossing their soft toys into the grid. The first person to form a line with his or her soft toys wins the game.

Pom Pom Sensory Bag

This pom pom bag activity is an easy way to create a mess-free, sensory and fine motor skill experience for children.

Prep time

15 mins

Clean-up time

5 mins

Materials

· 1-gallon Ziploc bag · 15 pom poms in 5 different colors · Clear hair gel or water · A piece of 30 cm by 30 cm cardboard (optional) · Painter's tape · Markers in the same five colors as the pom poms · Empty Grid printable on page 133 · Dotted Grid printable on page 134 · Sorting Mat printable on page 135

How to set up this activity for preschoolers

• Place all 15 pom poms into a Ziploc bag. Squeeze in some clear hair gel or pour in a cup of water.

• Place the Ziploc bag on top of the square cardboard. Tape three of the edges with painter's tape. Leave one of the edges open to slot in the printable. If you do not have cardboard, simply tape the bag down onto the table or the floor.

• Print a copy of the Dotted Grid printable. Color the circles with the five markers. Slot in this Dotted Grid printable behind the sensory bag.

• Invite your preschooler to push each pom pom to the circles with matching colors.

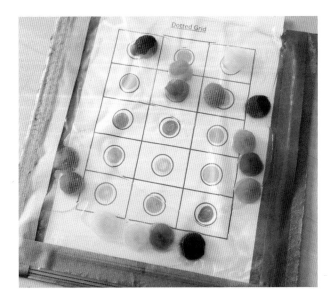

Variation for preschoolers

Print a copy of the Sorting Mat printable.

Write the numbers '1' to '5' in each circle and slot this behind the sensory bag. Invite your preschooler to count and push the pom poms into the circles according to the number.

How to simplify this activity for toddlers

- Print a copy of the Sorting Mat printable. Color the circles using the same five colors as the pom poms you have. Slot this behind the sensory bag.

- Invite your toddler to push the pom poms into the circles with the same color.

Variation for toddlers

Invite your toddler to line up the pom poms along the outlines of the circles.

How to extend this activity for school-aged kids

- Print a copy of the Empty Grid printable and slot it behind the sensory bag.
- Print a copy of the Dotted Grid printable. Color the circles with the five markers.

- Challenge your big kid to recreate the pattern on the Dotted Grid printable by pushing the pom poms to the spaces on the empty grid.

- If she completes the task easily, challenge her to create a symmetrical version of the Dotted Grid.

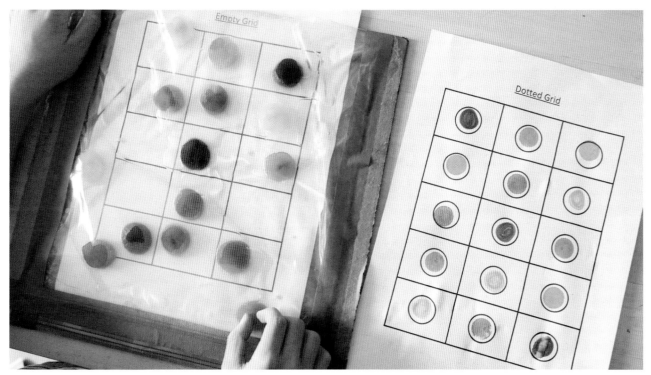

Fruit Stick Patterns

Through this playful and educational snack time activity, children learn basic patterns and develop fine motor skills while making fruit skewers.

Prep time

15 mins

Clean-up time

10 mins

Materials

- 3 types of fruits cut into small pieces
- Bamboo sticks

How to set up this activity for preschoolers

- Invite your preschooler to make fruit skewers by poking the fruits through the bamboo sticks.

- Introduce simple patterns like AB and AABB. Ask your child to arrange the fruits in AB or AABB patterns.

How to simplify this activity for toddlers

- Toddlers can use the same set up with the preschooler and create fruit skewers of any random pattern.

- If you do not feel comfortable letting your toddler handle bamboo sticks, give her a bowl of mixed fruits and task her to sort the fruits.

Tip

Do this activity during snack time. After the activity, your children can eat up these healthy fruits.

How to extend this activity for school-aged kids

- Challenge your school-aged kid to create fruit skewers using more complex patterns like ABC, AAB, AABC, etc.

Variation for everyone

Extend this activity into an engineering project. Challenge your children to build two-dimensional or three-dimensional shapes with fruits and bamboo sticks.

Chapter 6

Discovery of the World

Children are naturally curious about the world around them and they approach everyday experiences with so much excitement. At home, we can nurture our children's curiosity by providing opportunities for them to explore their environment, ask questions, and make discoveries. The ten activities in this section are designed to widen our children's knowledge of the world, particularly in the areas of geography, history, and science, through hands-on activities.

In Build the Longest Bridge (p. 64), children explore the concept of stability as they put their bridge to the test by balancing ten toys on it. Find the Path (p. 76) is an easy-to-grasp and playful activity that introduces the basic concepts of programming to young children. Even toddlers can participate in this one! In Wheels and Rolls (p. 78), children build fun rolling toys, and learn how wheels and axles work together to produce motion.

Ignite the joy of discovery in your children today!

Build the Longest Bridge

In this activity, children take on a fun engineering challenge:
to build the longest and strongest bridge that can hold ten toys on it.

Prep time

5 mins

Clean-up time

10 mins

Materials

- Popsicle sticks · Painter's tape
- Party cups
- 10 animal figurines/small toys

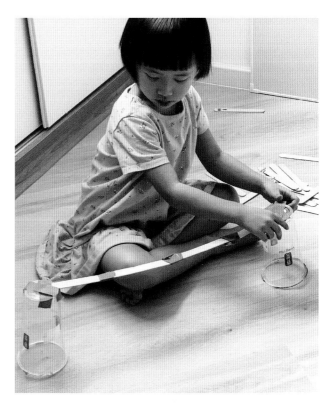

How to set up this activity for preschoolers

- Announce the challenge: Build the longest and strongest bridge for 10 animals to cross at the same time.

- Invite your children to come up with creative ways to build their bridges with the materials provided.

How to simplify this activity for toddlers

- Encourage your toddler to build simple bridges by balancing popsicle sticks across two cups.

- Challenge your toddler to balance as many toys as possible on the bridge.

How to extend this activity for school-aged kids

- Task your school-aged child to do research on famous bridges in the world, and share her findings with the family.

- Encourage your big kid to use one of the famous bridges she researched on as inspiration for building her longest bridge.

Fun fact

The world's longest bridge is the Danyang–Kunshan Grand Bridge in China which spans 102.4 miles (165 kilometers).

Variation for everyone

Make this a family project and invite everyone to work as a team to build the longest popsicle stick bridge ever.

Build the Tallest Structure

Using only markers and tape, children explore ways to build the tallest standing structure and learn basic concepts of structural engineering.

How to set up this activity for preschoolers

- Announce the challenge: Build the tallest structure that can stand.

- Invite your children to come up with creative ways to build a standing structure with markers and tape.

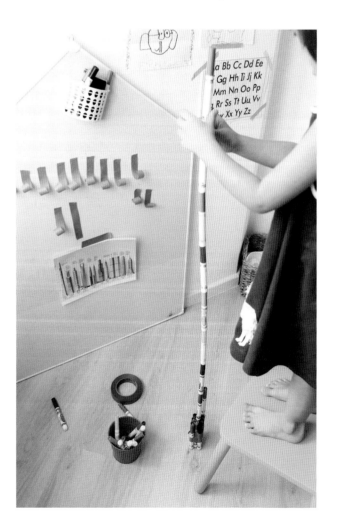

Prep time

5 mins

Clean-up time

10 mins

Materials

- Painter's tape
- 20 to 30 markers

How to simplify this activity for toddlers

- Instead of building a standing structure, invite your toddler to build shapes, like triangles, squares, and rectangles, with the markers and tape.

- Peel off a few pieces of tape and stick them along the edge of the table, to be used by your toddler.

Variation for toddlers

Challenge your toddler to attach the markers onto the wall using painter's tape.

How to extend this activity for school-aged kids

- Challenge your school-aged kid to come up with ways to measure the height of all the structures as accurately as possible.

- Invite her to do research on the five tallest structures in the world.

- Compare the heights of these mega buildings to the heights of their structures.

Variations for everyone

Here are three more ways to modify the activity and get your children excited about building again:

1. Use another building material. Some ideas include plastic spoons, popsicle sticks, straws, etc.

2. Challenge your children to build a standing structure that doesn't topple over when you hang a small toy at the top.

3. Finally, challenge your children to build a giant building or pyramid that can house ten of their stuffed animals.

Fun fact

The world's tallest structure is Burj Khalifa in Dubai, standing at 829.8-metre-tall (2,722 ft).

Map Your Room

This brilliant activity offers children an authentic map-making and map-reading experience.

Prep time

5 mins

Clean-up time

5 mins

Materials

· Paper · Markers · Three toys for hiding
· Washi tape (optional)

How to set up this activity for preschoolers

- Ask your preschooler to look around the room and list the furniture items she sees.

- Discuss where each item should be located on her map. Draw the furniture on the map together.

- Once the map is completed, invite her to hide three toys around the room.

- Ask her to mark Xs on the map to indicate where she has hidden the three toys.

- Exchange this "treasure map" with her sibling's. Siblings use each other's treasure maps to find the hidden toys.

- (optional) Mark the Xs with washi tape so that children can re-use their treasure maps.

How to simplify this activity for toddlers

- Your toddler can help hide the toys or find the toys during the treasure hunt.

- When it is her turn to hide the toys, you can help to indicate the locations of the hidden toys on the map drawn by her older sibling.

- Challenge your big kid to draw a map of a larger room or several rooms.

Fun fact

It is said that the first map of the world was drawn more than 2,600 years ago by a Greek philosopher named Anaximander. In his map, earth was a circle, with the lands grouped together in the center and the ocean all around.

Shadow Monsters

This is a wonderful invitation to have fun making shadows and to understand how they are formed.

Prep time

10 mins

Clean-up time

10 mins

Materials

• Large piece of white paper • A flashlight
• Random materials for building the shadow monsters. Here are some ideas: Small toys, bottles, paper cups, popsicle sticks, toilet rolls, bottle caps, clothes pegs, etc.
• Painter's tape

How to set up this activity for preschoolers

• Attach paper to an empty wall.

• Shine light on the paper. Invite your child to build monsters with the materials provided and observe the shadows that are cast on the wall.

• Invite him to trace the outline of his shadow monsters on the paper.

How to simplify this activity for toddlers

- Invite your toddler to create shadows on the walls with his favorite toys.

- Or, if your toddler is game, invite him to create a shadow monster, but help him tape together his creation by providing him with several pieces of tape, and by assisting him in tracing the outline of his monster.

How to extend this activity for school-aged kids

- Challenge your big kid to create a story involving his shadow monster. He can create props and act out his shadow play for his siblings.

Fun fact

Shadow puppetry originated in China and India more than two thousand years ago and is considered the oldest form of puppetry in the world.

Sink or Float?

All you need is water and some fruits, and your children are ready to learn about density.

Caution

Grapes are choking hazards. If young toddlers are doing this activity, use sliced grapes.

How to set up this activity for preschoolers

- Ask your child to predict whether each fruit will float or sink in water. Test his prediction by dropping each fruit in water.

- Ask your child to predict whether a peeled orange will float or sink. Let him peel an orange and test his prediction.

Prep time

10 mins

Clean-up time

15 mins

Materials

· A container of water · Ladles · Bowls · Three types of fruits (e.g., oranges, apples, and grapes) · Bamboo sticks

How to simplify this activity for toddlers

- Make this into a fun water-and-fruit sensory bin for your toddler. Give your toddler ladles and bowls to scoop the fruits and water into.

How to extend this activity for school-aged kids

- Give your big kid some bamboo sticks and challenge her to think of ways to make the grapes float. (Hint: use the orange peels)

Fun fact

An unpeeled orange floats because the peel of the orange is porous and filled with tiny air pockets, enabling it to float. When we peel the orange, we are removing all the air pockets, making the orange denser than water, thus causing it to sink.

Animal Ice Rescue

This activity provides endless sensory fun and introduces children to the concepts of freezing and melting.

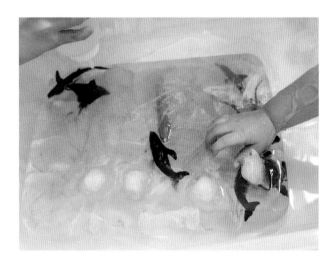

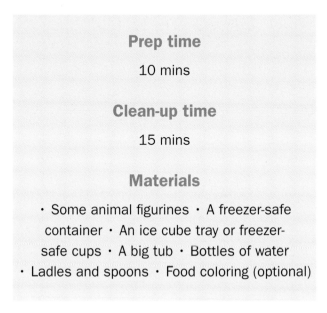

Prep time
10 mins

Clean-up time
15 mins

Materials

· Some animal figurines · A freezer-safe container · An ice cube tray or freezer-safe cups · A big tub · Bottles of water · Ladles and spoons · Food coloring (optional)

How to set up this activity for preschoolers

- Put the animal figurines in the freezer-safe container. Add water to cover the figurines and drop in some food coloring (optional). Freeze this container of water overnight. The next day, release the big block of ice from the container into the big tub. Add a little water.

- Invite your preschooler to carry out a rescue mission. Offer him the bottles of water, ladles, and spoons. Challenge him to rescue all the animals from the block of ice.

How to simplify this activity for toddlers

- For young toddlers, smaller blocks of ice are easier for them to handle. Freeze the animal figurines in an ice cube tray or in cups instead.

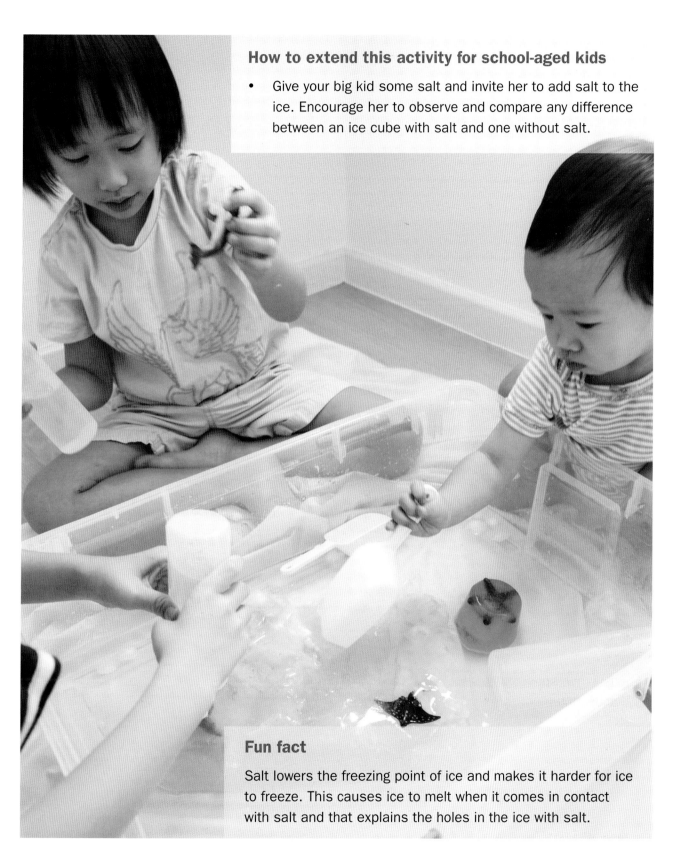

How to extend this activity for school-aged kids

- Give your big kid some salt and invite her to add salt to the ice. Encourage her to observe and compare any difference between an ice cube with salt and one without salt.

Fun fact

Salt lowers the freezing point of ice and makes it harder for ice to freeze. This causes ice to melt when it comes in contact with salt and that explains the holes in the ice with salt.

Find the Path

The visualization of steps as children find a path between the letters teaches them the basic concepts of programming.

How to set up this activity for preschoolers

- Draw arrows on 16 dot stickers.

- Using Find the Path Alphabet Grid and Find the Path Level 1, place an animal figurine on the first letter on the grid.

- Tell your preschooler that the animal is finding its way to the second letter. Challenge your preschooler to find a path between the two letters using the specific number of steps stated in the printable.

- Invite your preschooler to work through the rest of the challenges.

Prep time

10 mins

Clean-up time

5 mins

Materials

· Two animal figurines · Eight small bottle caps/pouch lids/tokens/coins · Dot stickers · Marker · Find the Path Alphabet Grid printable on page 136 · Find the Path Level 1, 2a, 2b, 3a, and 3b printables on pages 137–141

How to simplify this activity for toddlers

- Using Find the Path Alphabet Grid, place an animal figurine on a letter, e.g., 'I'. Place the second animal figurine on a second letter, e.g., 'L'. Choose pairs of letters where the path between them is a straight line and takes only one to three steps.

- Tell your toddler that the first animal is looking for the second animal. Challenge her to build a bridge using bottle caps between the two toys.

- Repeat this as many times as she likes with animal figurines on different letters.

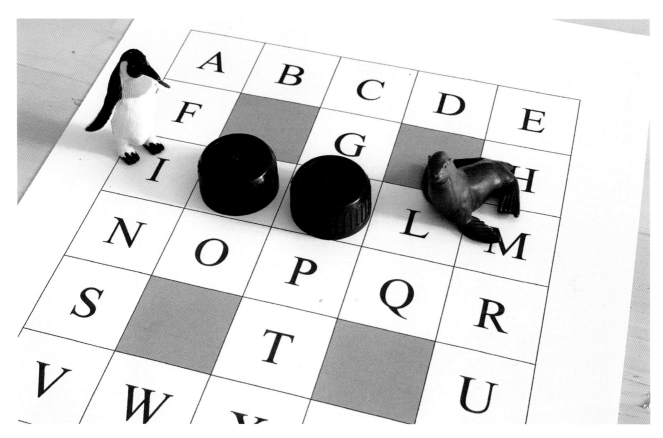

How to extend this activity for school-aged kids

- Draw arrows on 40 dot stickers.

- Using Find the Path Alphabet Grid and Find the Path Level 2a and 2b, challenge your big kid to find the path between the letters using the specific number of steps stated in the printable. He is to show the sequence of steps and directions, using the dot stickers.

- Challenge older school-aged children by using Find the Path Level 3a and 3b.

Fun fact

The first programmer in the world was a woman named Ada Lovelace.

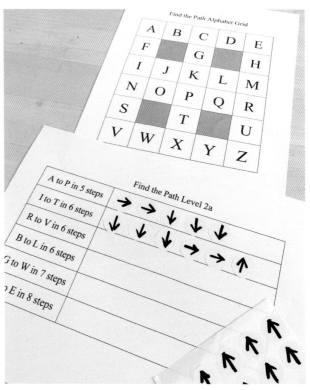

Wheels and Rolls

Here is an amazingly simple building project to make wheel-and-axle machines using cardboard and toilet paper rolls.

How to set up this activity for preschoolers

- Invite your child to decorate his cardboard circles and TP rolls with markers.

- An adult will have to do this step: Poke a tiny hole in the middle of the cardboard circles with scissors.

- To make a rolling toy with cardboard wheels, insert each end of a straw through each tiny hole in two cardboard wheels.

- To make a rolling toy with TP rolls, attach a TP roll to each end of the straw with tape.

- Make a race course ramp using the huge piece of cardboard.

Prep time

15 mins

Clean-up time

10 mins

Materials

· Cardboard cut into circles
· Toilet paper (TP) rolls that are cut in half
· Straws · Tape · Markers · Scissors
· A huge and long piece of cardboard

- Invite your preschooler to roll his rolling toys on the floor and down the ramp. Ask him these questions:

  Does your toy move faster on the floor or down the ramp?

  How can we make your toys roll faster?

How to simplify this activity for toddlers

- Your toddler will need your help to construct his rolling toys.

- As your toddler is playing with his rolling toys, ask him these questions:

  Which toy is faster?

  Which toy is slower?

  Which toy is the slowest or fastest?

How to extend this activity for school-aged kids

- Challenge your school-aged kid to improve the design of her rolling toy (e.g., by altering the size of the wheels or the length of the straw) to make it go faster.

- Set up an experiment to test the speed of her improved toy.

Fun fact

The oldest wheels were pottery wheels, invented about 5,500 years ago. Ancient Greeks figured out much later how to use wheels in transportation and invented the wheelbarrow.

Dot Sticker Constellations

Here's a hands-on activity that will spark your children's interest in constellations and stars, while helping them to learn about shapes at the same time.

How to set up this activity for preschoolers

- Explain to your child that a constellation is a group of stars that forms a shape in the sky.

- Draw stars on 30 dot stickers. Invite your child to stick the dot sticker stars on the gray dots on the Polygon Constellations printable, to create polygon-shaped constellations.

- Ask him to count the number of stars in each constellation.

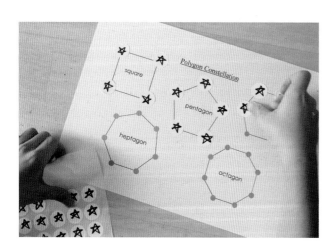

Variation for preschoolers

Ask your child to connect one dot to another with a marker, as a prewriting activity.

Prep time

10 mins

Clean-up time

5 mins

Materials

- Shape Constellations printable on page 142
- Polygon Constellations printable on page 143
- Dot stickers · A marker · Paper

How to simplify this activity for toddlers

- Draw stars on 19 dot stickers. Using the Shape Constellations printable, invite your toddler to stick the dot sticker stars on the gray dots to create constellations.

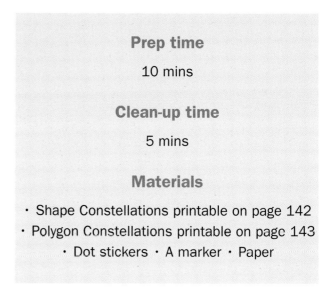

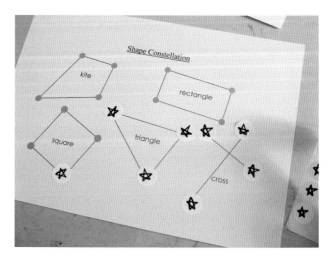

How to extend this activity for school-aged kids

- Task your big kid to do research on famous constellations.

- Draw and create these famous constellations with dot sticker stars.
- Or, encourage your big kid to create and name his own constellations.

Fun fact

Constellations are groups of stars that can be joined by imaginary lines to make pictures. There are 88 recognised constellations, and they are mostly named after mythological characters, animals, and objects.

sticker Igloo

This activity lends itself nicely to learning about igloos as children construct their igloos with tab stickers.

Tip

If you do not have tab stickers, cut small pieces of white paper and stick them with glue.

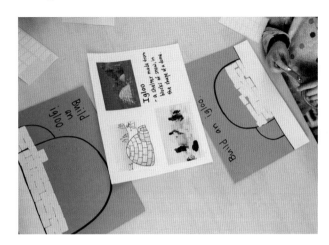

How to set up this activity for preschoolers

- Draw the outline of an igloo on the construction paper.

- Invite your child to create his igloo by using tab stickers as if they were blocks of snow. Challenge him to leave no gaps between the stickers.

How to simplify this activity for toddlers

- Invite your toddler to stick the tab stickers within the outline of the igloo. It is not important that your toddler's tab stickers are not aligned or stacked neatly.

Prep time

5 mins

Clean-up time

5 mins

Materials

- Tab stickers · Construction paper
- · Marker

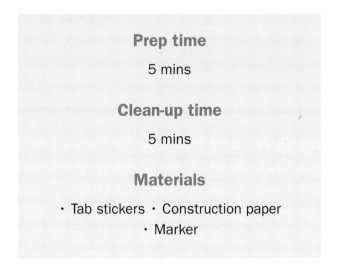

How to extend this activity for school-aged kids

- Task your school-aged kid to find out more about igloos and who lives in them. Invite him to share his findings with his siblings, before this activity.

Igloos were used as temporary winter shelters for the Inuit hunters' families during their hunting trips. Skilled Inuit hunters can build an igloo in less than an hour!

Build an igloo.

Chapter **7**

Motor Skills

Children love to move and are naturally motivated to develop their motor skills from birth. Gross motor skills, e.g., walking, balancing, jumping, and throwing, use larger muscles and involve large movements of the body. Fine motor skills, e.g., threading, pasting, cutting, and picking up small items, use smaller muscles, such as the muscles in the fingers, wrists, and hands. Mastery of motor skills in the early years is important as children need such skills to explore their environment and perform daily tasks.

Container Wagon Race (p. 86) is a fun-filled activity for children to work their hands and fingers. Children will be thrilled to race against each other using their homemade wagons. In Bottle Cap Table Carrom (p. 98), you'll transform your table into a carrom board! Children will experiment with strength and control as they push the bottle caps across but not over the table. Paper Plate Crazy Hair (p. 102) is a fine motor activity that encourages creativity and offers opportunity for children to practise cutting, tying, and weaving.

Choose an activity from this section and get everyone moving now!

container Wagon Race

Children will love the adrenaline rush of racing with their DIY wagons.

Prep time

10 mins

Clean-up time

5 mins

Materials

· Plastic food containers · String (6.5ft or around 2m long) · Plastic bottles or cardboard rolls · Tape · Stickers or permanent markers to decorate the wagons · Stuffed toys as passengers in the wagons (optional)

How to set up this activity for preschoolers

- Invite your preschooler to decorate the food container with stickers or markers.

- Guide her to tape one end of the string to the bottle and the other end of the string to the food container.

- Turn the bottle to pull in the food container wagon.

- Encourage your child to have a race with her siblings to see who can pull in her wagon in the shortest amount of time.

How to simplify this activity for toddlers

- Use a shorter string (5ft or 1.5m long) for toddlers.

- Invite your toddler to join in the race or simply have fun pulling her stuffed toys around the house in her wagon.

How to extend this activity for school-aged kids

- Task your big kid to record the time for his siblings to complete the wagon race with a stopwatch.

- Join in the fun and challenge your big kid to a wagon race!

Follow the Lines

Here's a simple activity to get your children to move about and expend some energy at home!

How to set up this activity for preschoolers

- Using the painter's tape or washi tape, form three long lines on the floor, e.g., a straight line, a zigzag line, and a castle line.

- Challenge your preschooler to do the following actions along the lines:

  - Walk

  - Walk backwards

  - Hop with two feet

  - Hop on one foot

  - Hop backwards

  - Walk with feet on one line and hands on another line

  - Tiptoe

  - Jump from one line to another

How to simplify this activity for toddlers

- No variation is required. Invite your toddler to attempt the same actions as the preschoolers and have fun together.

How to extend this activity for school-aged kids

- Ask your older child to think of more challenging actions, like balancing a book on his head, holding two balls in his hands, or holding a spoon with pom poms while walking along the lines.

Variation for everyone

Put on some music and
invite everyone to have
fun dancing while travelling
along the lines!

Blindfold Rescue

This is a collaborative game where siblings are the 'eyes' for each other and they have to guide each other to complete the rescue mission.

Prep time

5 mins

Clean-up time

5 mins

Materials

· Painter's tape · Markers
· Blindfolds

How to set up this activity for preschoolers

- Using painter's tape, paste markers all over a wall at different heights.

- Introduce basic directions, like up, down, left, and right, to your child.

- Blindfold him.

- Call out a color. The other sibling gives instructions to direct the blindfolded child to the wall to retrieve the correct marker.

- Children take turns to be blindfolded or to give directions.

How to simplify this activity for toddlers

- Attach some markers at the toddler's height.

- Ask the older sibling to hold the toddler's hand and lead her to the wall.

- Younger toddlers can ditch the blindfold and simply have fun grabbing the markers off the wall.

How to extend this activity for school-aged kids

- Move some markers higher and lower, so that your big kid has to stretch, squat, or even jump to reach the markers.

- Ask the younger sibling to direct his big brother or sister to retrieve all the markers on the wall.

Variations for everyone

Spin your children around a few times before the start of the game.

Or, before blindfolding, ask everyone to look at the wall for ten seconds and remember the positions of the markers. Without any directions, challenge your blindfolded children to work together to retrieve all the markers on the wall as quickly as possible.

Shaker Bottles

This simple activity develops fine motor skills in many ways as children get to peel, paste, scoop, and pour.

How to set up this activity for preschoolers

*   Invite your preschooler to decorate his shaker bottle with washi tape and stickers.

*   Fold a small piece of paper into a cone. Snip off the end to make a hole. Invite your preschooler to use this paper cone as a funnel for filling the bottles with small items.

*   Then, after sealing the bottle, encourage him to sing and dance with his homemade musical shaker.

How to simplify this activity for toddlers

*   Use a bottle with a bigger opening for your toddler.

*   Offer her bigger filler items, like cut-up straws, aluminum sticks, and penne pasta, as the fillers for her shaker bottle.

How to extend this activity for school-aged kids

- Task your school-aged kid to find out more about rain sticks and where they originate from. Invite him to share his findings with his siblings, before this activity.

- Challenge your big kid to make a rain stick with a cardboard tube and think of ways to slow down the flow of the fillers inside the cardboard tube. This will produce a longer raindrop sound. Here's an idea: Seal one end of the tube with masking tape. Roll up aluminum foil into a long stick and twist it into a coil. Insert the aluminum coil into the tube. Pour in the fillers and seal the other end with masking tape.

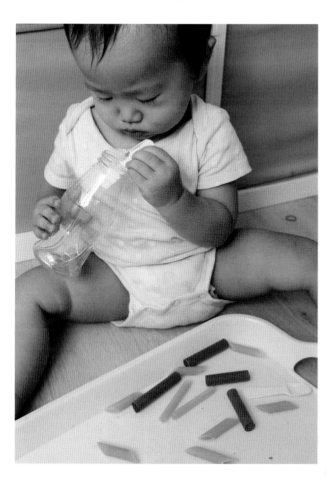

Variation for everyone

Play a fun music game with the shakers. Children can take turns to shout 'louder', 'softer', 'faster', slower', 'higher', 'lower', 'front', and 'back', and everyone will shake their shakers or rain sticks according to the instruction.

Paper Plate Web

Weaving and threading are wonderful ways for children to build fine motor skills and develop hand-eye coordination.

Prep time

15 mins

Clean-up time

10 mins

Materials

· Paper plates (6in or 15cm in diameter)
· Hole puncher · Yarn · Pipe cleaners
· Scissors · Marker

- Invite your preschooler to make a spider web for the spider by threading the yarn through the holes and across the paper plate. When he runs out of yarn, tie another piece of yarn to the old one.

How to simplify this activity for toddlers

- For toddlers, offer a shorter piece of yarn (around 2ft or 0.6m long). Young toddlers may like to simply wrap the yarn around the paper plate and not thread through the holes.

How to set up this activity for preschoolers

- Punch holes all around the paper plate and draw a spider in the center.

- Cut a piece of yarn that is about 3ft or 1m long.

- Secure one end of the yarn to one of the holes on the paper plate.

- Make a small needle using pipe cleaner (see photo) and tie the other end of the yarn to this pipe cleaner needle.

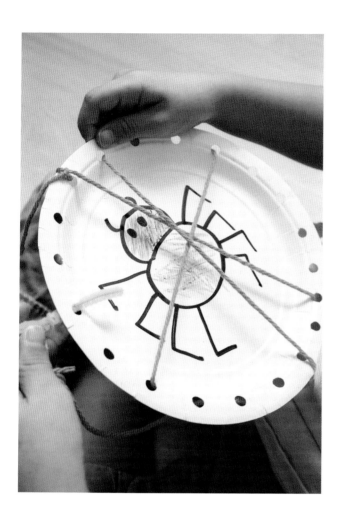

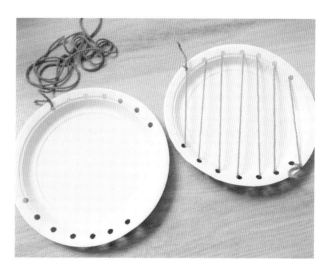

How to extend this activity for school-aged kids

- Create seven vertical lines across the paper plate with the yarn.

- Cut a long piece of yarn around 3ft or 1m long. Tie one end of the yarn to the top of the first vertical line. Invite your child to weave through the lines by bringing the yarn over and under the vertical lines. When he reaches the last line, loop back and continue weaving.

- When he is done weaving, simply tie the yarn to one of the vertical lines and cut away the excess yarn.

Variation for everyone

Write numbers near each hole. Challenge your children to thread the yarn through the holes, from the smallest to the biggest number.

Fill the House

Introduce your children to the concept of area while getting them to search around the house.

Prep time

10 mins

Clean-up time

10 mins

Materials

· Painter's tape · Toys, books, and other items around the house · Paper · Scissors

How to set up this activity for preschoolers

- Make an outline of a house on the floor with painter's tape.

- Invite your child to search around and fill the house outline with toys, books, and other items, leaving as few gaps in between as possible.

How to simplify this activity for toddlers

- As your toddler picks up items to fill the house, ask him to name the shape of the item in his hands.

How to extend this activity for school-aged kids

- Measure and cut several pieces of 5-by-5 inch or 10-by-10 cm square paper. Challenge your big kid to estimate the area of the house with the paper.

Bottle Cap Table Carrom

Through this game, children develop control of their hand and arm strength.

How to set up this activity for preschoolers

- Using painter's tape, make five horizontal lines on a table, as shown in the photo.

- Make two more short vertical lines at the top corners of the table. These lines create the different scoring zones and the starting line.

- Assign different scores to each zone. The area furthest from your child and closest to the edge of the table gets the highest score.

- Invite your child to slide his bottle caps across the table.

- He scores the points where his bottle caps stop. He scores zero if the bottle caps fall off the table.

How to simplify this activity for toddlers

- If your toddler finds it challenging to push the bottle caps, use toy cars instead. Invite her to push her toy cars across the table, but not over the table.

How to extend this activity for school-aged kids

- Challenge your big kid to aim for the zones at the corners of the table with the highest score.

- Task your big kid to record and compute the scores for everyone.

Variation for everyone

Create a giant version of this game on the floor! Create boxes of different sizes using painter's tape. The smallest box has the highest score while the biggest box has the lowest score. Instead of using bottle caps, have your children push toy cars or toss soft toys into the boxes.

Dot Sticker Ice Cream

Dot stickers are amazing for working small finger muscles and making learning fun and hands-on.

Prep time

10 mins

Clean-up time

5 mins

Materials

· Ice Cream Cones printable on page 144
· Markers · Dot stickers in five colors

How to set up this activity for preschoolers

- On the Ice Cream Cones printable, number the ice cream cones '1' to '5'.

- Invite your preschooler to paste dot stickers on the cones, as if they were scoops of ice cream, according to the numbers on the cones.

- If you don't have dot stickers, your child can use finger paint to make the scoops of ice cream.

Ice Cream Cones

How to simplify this activity for toddlers

- Color-code the cones according to the five dot sticker colors.

- Invite your toddler to match the colors of the dot stickers to that of the cones and paste the dot stickers on the matching cones.

How to extend this activity for school-aged kids

- Write different prices in the circles of each ice cream cone.

- Allocate a price to each dot sticker color.

- Invite your big kid to create 'ice cream' with dot stickers while making sure that the total price on the dot stickers matches the total price on each cone.

Variation for school-aged kids

Write addition or subtraction problems on the cones and challenge your big kid to paste the number of dot stickers that corresponds to the answers.

Paper Plate Crazy Hair

**This is a fun way to invite children to practise cutting.
Children will love being hairstylists for the day.**

Prep time

10 mins

Clean-up time

10 mins

Materials

· Paper plates · Markers · Scissors
· Construction paper or old magazine paper
· Tape or glue · Rubber bands or ribbons

How to set up this activity for preschoolers

- Give a paper plate to your child and invite him to draw a face on it.

- Attach big strips of paper above the face.

- Offer your child a pair of scissors and ask your child to cut the paper into thinner strips to create 'hair'.

- Tell your child that he is a hair stylist. Invite him to cut a new hairstyle for his paper plate face.

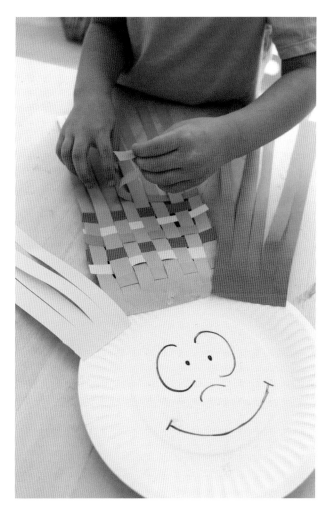

How to simplify this activity for toddlers

- Draw the face for your toddler.

- Draw lines on the big strips of paper and invite your toddler to cut along the lines to create 'hair'.

- For young toddlers, cut the paper into thinner strips, then invite them to tear the strips to create a new hairstyle.

How to extend this activity for school-aged kids

- Offer rubber bands or ribbons to your big kid and challenge him to create interesting hairdos.

- Invite your big kid to weave or braid the paper hair.

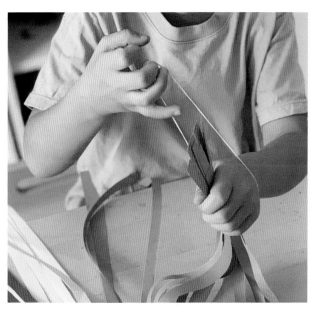

Giant Pom Pom Run

This building activity develops manual dexterity and problem solving skills.

Prep time

5 mins

Clean-up time

10 mins

Materials

· Toilet paper rolls · Kitchen rolls
· Strips of cardboard (optional)
· Painter's tape · Pom poms

How to set up this activity for preschoolers

- Invite your child to create a pom pom run by sticking the rolls on a wall.

- He can adjust the rolls to connect smoothly with the next one, taping them to the wall with painter's tape.

- Put some pom poms through the rolls and observe if they flow through smoothly.

- When a pom pom gets stuck in a roll, adjust it and test the pom pom run again.

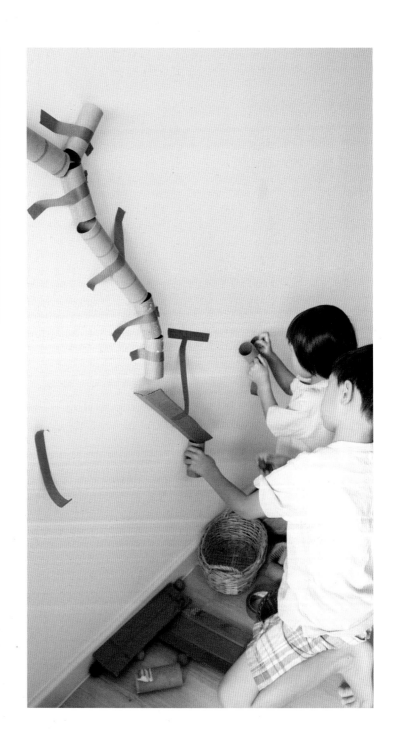

How to simplify this activity for toddlers

- Attach a few rolls at a lower height for your toddler.

- Invite your toddler to pick and drop pom poms through these rolls or through the pom pom run created by her older siblings.

How to extend this activity for school-aged kids

- Challenge your school-aged kid to design and build a super long pom pom run.

- Offer strips of cardboard for your big kid to create ramps for his pom pom run.

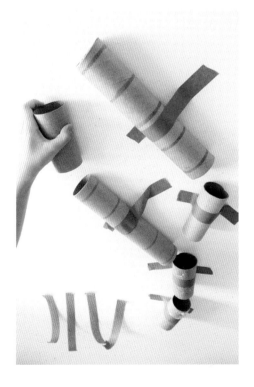

Chapter 8

Sensory Play, Arts and crafts

Experiences in sensory play, art and crafts have tremendous positive effects on children's development. As children engage in sensory play, they actively use their five senses to explore their environment, helping them to make sense of the world and build neural connections in their brains. Arts and crafts provide creative means for children to express themselves and develop their imaginations. When children use paint and glue, they are also developing their fine motor skills and hand-eye coordination. Children who are encouraged to be creative also develop a strong sense of confidence.

In Big Body Art (p. 110), children create life-size drawings of themselves. I guarantee this is one art project they will never forget. Box Houses (p. 120) is a fun collaborative activity for siblings to design their dream houses together. Vegetable Soup (p. 124) is a low-prep sensory-filled activity for children to explore the texture, color, and smell of various vegetables and fruits.

Have fun creating and playing together!

Paint the Bathroom

This messy painting experience in the bathroom is one your children will ask for again and again.

Tip

Do this activity before shower time and send the children to shower right after.

How to set up this activity for preschoolers

- Invite your preschooler to paint parts of the bathroom, e.g., the glass door of the shower area, bath tub, basin, bathroom floor, plastic storage container, etc. Choose an area that's easy to wash down after.

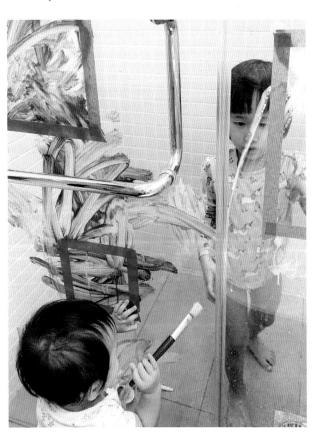

Prep time

10 mins

Clean-up time

10 mins

Materials

· Washable paint · Paint brushes
· Containers for paint
· Sponges (optional) · Hand soap (optional)

- After painting, task him to wash the bathroom with sponges and hand soap (optional).

How to simplify this activity for toddlers

- If you are uncomfortable with your toddler handling paint, try taste-safe paint made with yogurt and food coloring.

- Or, simply let your toddler paint with colored water (use a little food coloring) and a paintbrush.

- If you have a glass door in your bathroom, let the older siblings paint in the shower area and close the glass door. The toddler can paint on the other side of the glass door (see photo).

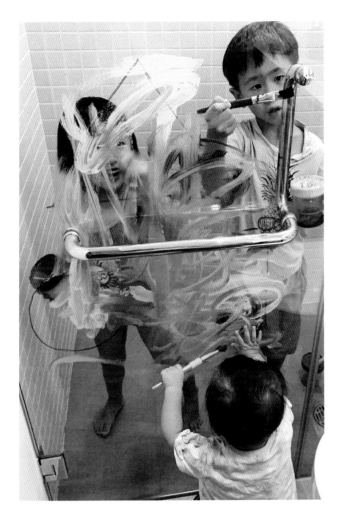

How to extend this activity for school-aged kids

- No variation is required. Your school-aged child will enjoy this open-ended art activity as much as her younger siblings.

Variation for everyone

Create frames on your bathroom door with painter's tape. Invite your children to create their paintings within these frames.

Big Body Art

This super fun experience is great for bringing siblings together to create amazing life-size art.

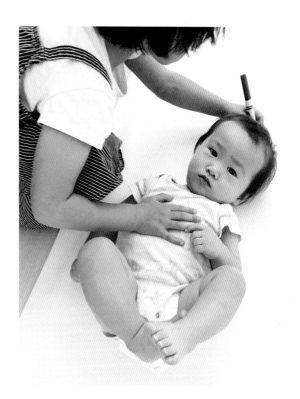

Prep time

10 mins

Clean-up time

5 mins

Materials

· Markers · Stickers
· Huge pieces of paper (the paper has to be bigger than your children)

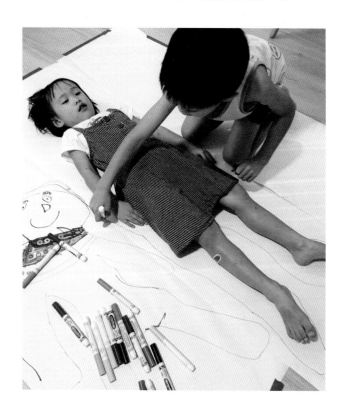

Tip

If you can't find huge pieces of paper, tape a few pieces of paper together or do this activity on a clear glass door.

How to set up this activity for preschoolers

• Tape huge pieces of paper on the floor. Ask one child to lie down on the paper and have an older sibling or an adult trace the outline of her body.

• Invite your preschooler to draw her face and an outfit for her body outline.

How to simplify this activity for toddlers

- Have your toddler lie down on the paper and ask an older sibling or adult to trace the outline of his body.

- Invite your toddler to decorate the outfit for his body outline with stickers and markers.

How to extend this activity for school-aged kids

- The older sibling helps to trace the outline of the body for her younger siblings.

- Invite your big kid to design an outfit for her body outline with interesting materials she can find around the house.

- Or, challenge her to conduct research from books or the Internet, and draw the digestive system of the body within the body outline.

Fruit Faces

Here's a creative snack time activity that uses fruits to create cute faces.

Prep time

15 mins

Clean-up time

10 mins

Materials

· Different types of fruits (e.g., blueberries, strawberries, and grapes) cut into small pieces
· Big, round slices of apples

Tip

Don't forget to take some photos of your children's creations before they end up in their tummies!

How to set up this activity for preschoolers

- Offer your preschooler some big, round apple slices.

- Invite him to add facial features to this apple 'face', using other fruits.

How to simplify this activity for toddlers

- Do this activity with your toddler, naming the parts of a face as you go along. For example, when adding the eyes, say, "These are the eyes. Where are your eyes? Can you point to your eyes?"

How to extend this activity for school-aged kids

- Challenge your big kid to create outfits for her fruit faces with fruits too.

- Or, make some animal faces with the fruits.

Variation for everyone

Offer some toothpicks to your children and challenge them to create three-dimensional fruit figures.

container Portrait

Siblings will love this fun collaborative art project where they get to draw each other's portrait on a container!

How to set up this activity for preschoolers

- Have a sibling hold a container in front of his face. Invite your preschooler to trace and draw his face on the container with a marker.

- The children switch their roles.

How to simplify this activity for toddlers

- Your toddler can join in this activity and have her container portrait drawn by her older sibling.

- If your toddler likes to draw too, offer her dry-erase markers instead.

- You can trace over her lines with the permanent marker after she is done drawing.

How to extend this activity for school-aged kids

- Challenge your big kid to pay attention to the small details on the face, like the eyebrows, eyelashes, etc.

- He can also add hair to his container portrait using strips of paper and double-sided tape.

- Offer your big kid a pair of scissors and encourage him to cut a new hairstyle for his container face.

Prep time

5 mins

Clean-up time

5 mins

Materials

· Large clear containers
· Permanent markers or dry-erase markers
· Construction paper · Scissors
· Double-sided tape

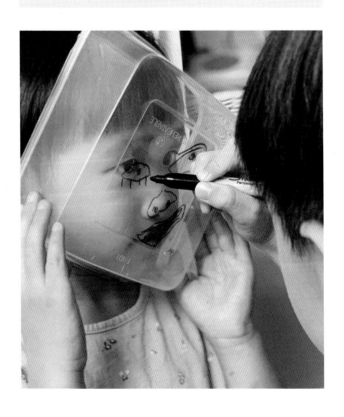

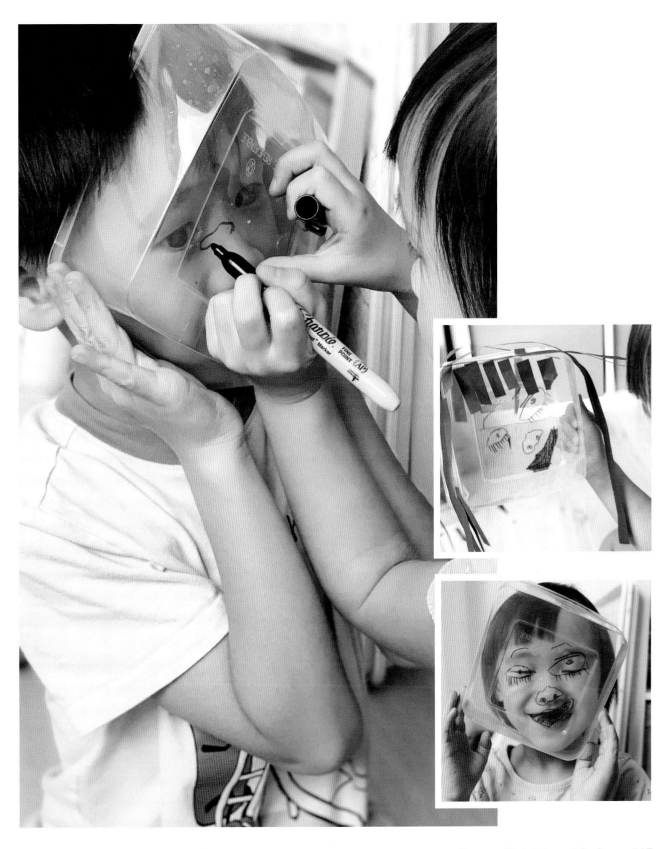

color wheel

Color mixing never fails to mesmerize children who are always thrilled to create new colors!

Prep time

10 mins

Clean-up time

10 mins

Materials

· Paper · Paint · Brushes
· Container of water · Permanent marker
· Ruler · Big round container or bowl
· Zipper storage bag

How to set up this activity for preschoolers

- Using the permanent marker, draw a big circle in the middle of the paper by tracing the outline of the container or bowl. Divide the circle into six equal parts.

- Invite your child to paint three sectors of the color wheel with the primary colors (red, blue, yellow), leaving a space between each sector.

- Invite him to mix two primary colors together and observe what happens.

- Paint the space between the two primary colors with the newly created color. Repeat for the other pairs of primary colors.

How to simplify this activity for toddlers

- For very young toddlers, squeeze two primary colors into a zipper storage bag. Invite your toddler to use her fingers to mix the paint in the bag.

- If you are comfortable with your older toddler handling paint, offer her paint in the three primary colors and paper. Encourage her to use the brushes to paint and explore what happens when she mixes these primary colors together.

How to extend this activity for school-aged kids

- Challenge your big kid to create the six tertiary colors by mixing secondary colors with primary colors. The six tertiary colors are yellow-orange, red-orange, red-purple, blue-purple, blue-green, and yellow-green.

Tie Dye Paper Towel

This is an invitation for children to create beautiful tie dye prints and explore the solubility of inks in water.

Tip

Encourage your children to apply color generously all over the paper towels for vivid effects.

How to set up this activity for preschoolers

- Invite your preschooler to fold the paper towels in half or into quarters, or roll the paper towels.

- Color the folded paper towels with washable markers. Using spoons or droppers, add water on the paper towels. Observe how the marker ink spreads when water is added.

- Carefully unfold the paper towels and lay them to air-dry.

How to simplify this activity for toddlers

- Toddlers may skip the folding and rolling step.

- Offer spoons instead of droppers to your toddler and ask her to wet the paper towels by scooping water over them.

Prep time

10 mins

Clean-up time

10 mins

Materials

· Washable markers · Paper towels
· Small container of water
· Small spoons or droppers · Rubber bands

How to extend this activity for school-aged kids

- Invite your big child to experiment with different ways to fold, twist, and tie their paper towels with rubber bands.

- Introduce the concept of solubility to your school-aged child. The ink from the washable markers is soluble in water. When water is added, the ink dissolves in the water and runs along the fibers in the paper towels.

Box Houses

Have a peek into your children's dream houses in this creative three-dimensional art project.

Prep time

15 mins

Clean-up time

10 mins

Materials

· A big box · Big pieces of paper · Tape · Permanent marker · Coloring tools, like washable markers, dot paint markers, paint sticks, tempera paint etc.

How to set up this activity for preschoolers

- Attach big pieces of paper on every side of the big box using tape.

- Draw outlines of big houses with windows and doors on the paper.

- Encourage your preschooler to imagine what his dream house looks like. Invite him to color or paint his dream house.

How to simplify this activity for toddlers

- Provide toddler-friendly coloring materials, like washable markers, paint sticks, and dot paint markers.

How to extend this activity for school-aged kids

- Leave the paper blank and invite your big kid to draw the house, windows and door, and fill in with colors.

- On one of the sides of the box, challenge him to draw the details of the inside of the house, e.g., the furniture and people inside the rooms. He could even add dialogue boxes above the people who are having conversations!

Kusama Hearts

Inspired by Japanese artist Yayoi Kusama and her famous dot paintings, children explore using only dots to create interesting art works.

Tip

No dot stickers or dot paint markers at home? Find a wine cork and use it like a stamp to stamp on paint dots.

Prep time

10 mins

Clean-up time

10 mins

Materials

· Paper · Black marker
· Dot paint markers or dot stickers
· Cotton buds · Rubber bands
· Tempera paint

How to set up this activity for preschoolers

- Use the marker to draw hearts of various sizes on the paper.

- Invite your preschooler to fill the hearts and the whole paper with dots using dot stickers or dot paint markers.

How to simplify this activity for toddlers

- No variation is required. Toddlers will enjoy this simple art project with their older siblings.

How to extend this activity for school-aged kids

- Challenge your big kid to create the dots with cotton buds and paint.

- Bundle six cotton buds together with a rubber band and your child can create several dots at once.

- Research about the Japanese artist, Yayoi Kusama, and her fascinating dot paintings.

Vegetable Soup

Save all the food scraps from your kitchen for this activity that will give your children hours of sensory and pretend play fun!

Prep time

5 mins

Clean-up time

10 mins

Materials

· Vegetable and fruit scraps · A big tub · Scoops and ladles · Bowls · Scissors (optional) · Paper and marker (optional)

How to set up this activity for preschoolers

- Fill half of the tub with water. Set out the scoops, ladles, bowls, and vegetable and fruit scraps.

- Invite your child to cook some 'vegetable soup'.

- For older preschoolers, offer them a pair of scissors to practise their cutting skills by cutting the ingredients.

How to simplify this activity for toddlers

* No variation is required. Toddlers will have fun in this sensory-filled pretend play activity.

How to extend this activity for school-aged kids

* Task your big kid to write a menu for the 'restaurant', with the soup names and prices.

* Your school-aged kid can pretend to be the waiter and take orders from customers like yourself.

Wacky Faces

This collaborative art project to draw some wacky faces together is guaranteed to entertain everyone!

Prep time

5 mins

Clean-up time

5 mins

Materials

· Sticky notes · Paper · Markers

How to set up this activity for preschoolers

- Draw outlines of faces on the paper. Prepare one face for every child.

- Cover the faces with sticky notes and give one face to each child.

- Invite him to peel off one sticky note and draw in a feature on the face, e.g., an eye, nose, mouth, or ears.

- Cover it with the sticky note and put a cross on the sticky note.

- Have the siblings pass their papers to each other.

- Repeat the process until every sticky note on every piece of paper has a cross.

- Invite everyone to peel off all the sticky notes and check out the wacky faces they drew together!

This simpler variation is good for young toddlers who are not into drawing yet: Draw two eyes, one nose, one mouth, and two ears on the sticky notes. Invite your toddler to stick these notes on a blank face.

How to extend this activity for school-aged kids

- Invite your big kid to lead his siblings in creating names for the wacky faces, and a story using the faces as characters. Encourage him to act out his story.

- Or, create fun variations like monsters, houses, or dresses, etc.

How to simplify this activity for toddlers

- Go through the parts of a face with your toddler and encourage your toddler to join in the activity.

- It doesn't matter if your toddler draws the eye at the wrong position or draws a nose inaccurately.

- At the end of the activity, invite him to compare the face on the paper and his own face in the mirror.

About the Author

Fynn is the creative brain behind *Happy Tot Shelf*, a hugely popular website that champions playful, hands-on learning to nurture the love of learning in children. Intrigued with all things related to Math, Science and Education, she pursued a Bachelor of Engineering (Chemical Engineering) and a Post-Graduate Diploma in Education, and was a Math and Science teacher for several years before deciding to stay home full-time with her children.

Watching her children grow up, Fynn was constantly awed at how they loved to learn from the time they were born. Determined to nurture this deep love of learning, she transferred her passion and experience in education to creating enriching learning activities for her children. She has a natural knack of making fun, hands-on activities using household items and recyclable materials.

Through *Happy Tot Shelf*, Fynn shares her creative learning ideas with parents so that they can raise happy little learners too. *Happy Tot Shelf* has amassed over 300,000 followers across various social media platforms and her posts and videos have been viewed and liked by millions of people. Fynn has been featured on the air, in print, and on various websites as an expert in creative learning ideas and as an enthusiastic proponent of learning through play.

Fynn lives in Singapore with her husband and three children.

You can find more creative learning ideas on her website happytotshelf.com, Instagram at @happytotshelf or Facebook facebook.com/happytotshelf.

Acknowledgements

To my amazing community of readers and followers of *Happy Tot Shelf*, thank you for every comment, message, question, and answer that gave me the inspiration for this book.

To my one and only editor, Ruth Wan, thank you for tending to this book with so much attention and wisdom, and making this book come to life with me.

To the entire World Scientific Publishing team, especially Hong Koon, Jimmy, Daniele, and Ugena, thank you for believing in my idea and putting the book together so quickly and seamlessly.

A special shoutout to my friend Lianne Ong, who generously shared her experience and opened up the world of book publishing to me.

To all my fellow Instagram creators, thank you for all the inspiration, support, and friendship. I am especially grateful to Abigail, Jacinth, and Jules for all the encouragement and late-night pep talks when I needed them most.

To my parents-in-law, thank you for loving my children and always being there for my family.

To Zachary, Riley, and Abby, you are the source of my joy and pride. There is nothing I would not do to fill your lives with love, smiles, and ice cream. I love you with every beat of my heart.

Lastly, this book would not exist were it not for the unwavering support and love of my best friend and husband, Shuhong. Thank you for reminding me of my value and worth every single day. Thank you for loving our children and me unconditionally. Thank you for always giving me the last potato chip in the bag. You are simply the best thing that has happened to me.

Shape Hunt Table

Shape	Number
⬤	
♡	
▢	
△	
▭	

Shape Hunt Graph

10					
9					
8					
7					
6					
5					
4					
3					
2					
1					
	○	♡	□	△	▭

Empty Grid

Dotted Grid

Sorting Mat

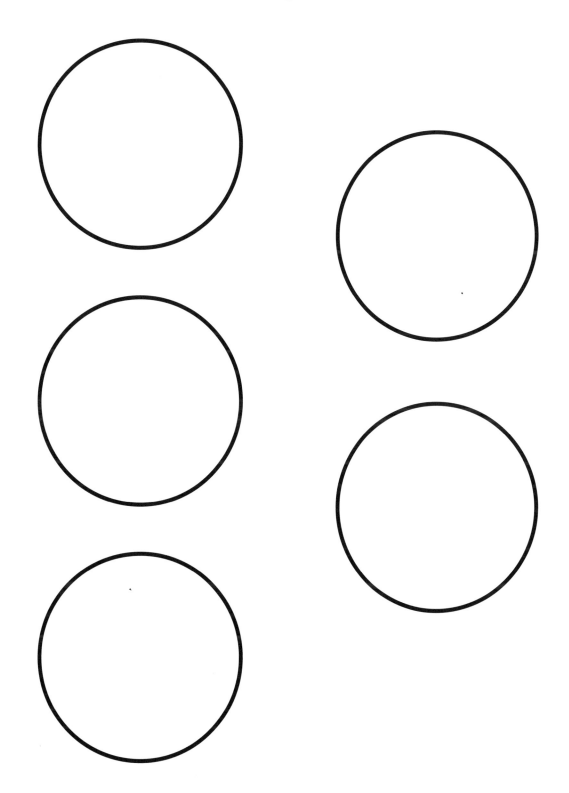

Find the Path Alphabet Grid

A	B	C	D	E
F		G		H
I	J	K	L	M
N	O	P	Q	R
S		T		U
V	W	X	Y	Z

Find the Path Level 1

F to J in 2 steps	K to T in 2 steps	V to X in 2 steps	M to Z in 3 steps	C to L in 3 steps	T to I in 4 steps

Find the Path Level 2a

A to P in 5 steps	I to T in 6 steps	R to V in 6 steps	B to L in 6 steps	G to W in 7 steps	Y to E in 8 steps

Find the Path Level 2b

E to L in 5 steps	J to U in 5 steps	N to H in 6 steps	P to D in 6 steps	B to U in 7 steps	X to G in 8 steps

Find the Path Level 3a

B to E in 7 steps	K to X in 7 steps	U to L in 8 steps	W to B in 8 steps	H to F in 8 steps	G to T in 9 steps

Find the Path Level 3b

H to A in 7 steps	J to T in 7 steps	M to S in 8 steps	B to X in 8 steps	K to L in 9 steps	Y to F in 9 steps

Shape Constellations

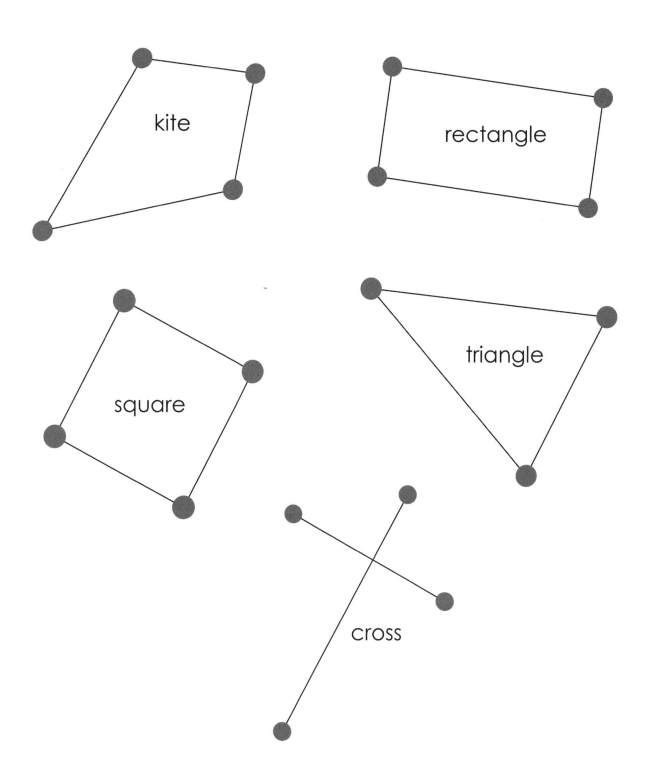

kite

rectangle

square

triangle

cross

Polygon Constellations

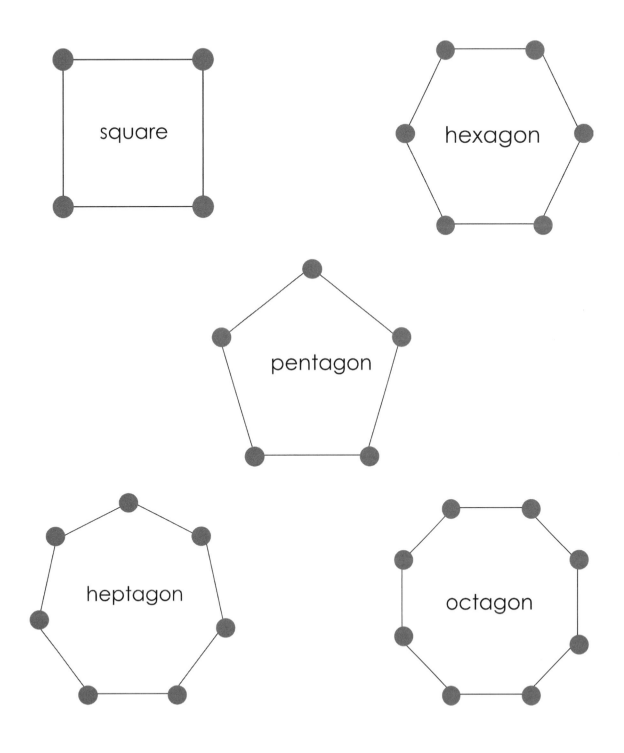

Ice Cream Cones

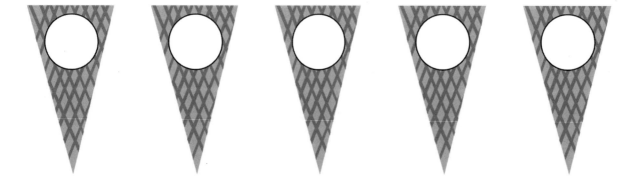